COVENA

The story of personal and church covenants
and their lessons for today

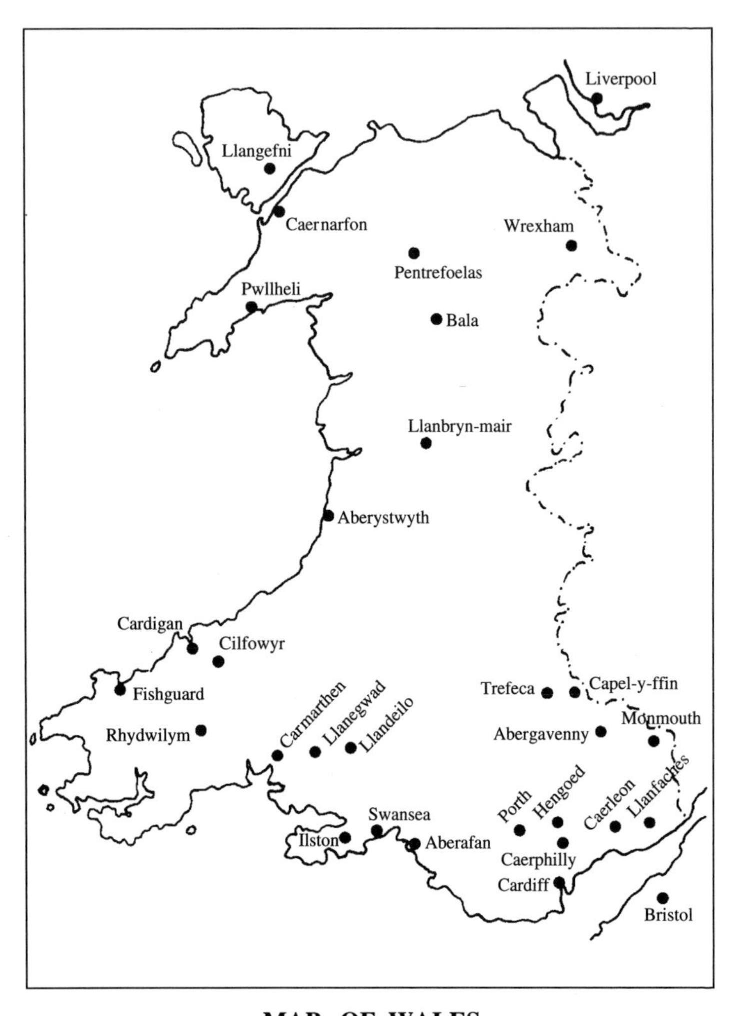

MAP OF WALES

(showing places mentioned in the book)

Covenanting with God

The story of personal and church covenants and their lessons for today

Gwyn Davies

Evangelical Library of Wales

First published, 1994

ISBN 1 85049 102 X

This book is an expanded version of the Annual English Lecture of the Evangelical Library of Wales for 1982, delivered in Aberystwyth in August 1982 during the Annual English Conference of the Evangelical Movement of Wales.

Cover design by Rhiain M. Davies (Cain)

Published by the Evangelical Library of Wales
Bryntirion, Bridgend, Mid Glamorgan, CF31 4DX, Wales
Printed in Wales by D. Brown & Sons Ltd, Bridgend

CONTENTS

ACKNOWLEDGEMENTS

I am indebted to a number of people for their assistance in the preparation of this volume. In particular, I should like to acknowledge the admirable service provided by the staff of the library at the University of Wales, Aberystwyth (and Elgan Davies in particular) and by the staff of the National Library of Wales at Aberystwyth; the helpful suggestions supplied by Noel A. Gibbard, Bobi Jones, and Gordon Macdonald; and the immaculate preparation of the typescript by Mrs Myfanwy Evans. I am also grateful to Edmund T. Owen for his assistance with the index and Dr Christine James for her help with the map. Special thanks are due to E. Wyn James, Librarian of the Evangelical Library of Wales, for inviting me to deliver the lecture on which this book is based and for seeing the work through the press. The encouragement given by my partner in the marriage covenant has been, as always, invaluable.

NOTE

The spelling and punctuation of original covenants quoted in the text have been modernized in order to make them more immediately intelligible. Covenants in the Appendices, on the other hand, have been reproduced verbatim from the sources noted.

INTRODUCTION

One of the most encouraging developments over the last few decades has been a renewed interest in covenant theology. Long neglected or altogether abandoned, the doctrine that 'God from eternity made a gracious covenant or plan, ordered in all things and sure, for the salvation of men'[1] has become increasingly attractive to a new generation of Christians anxious to avoid the heresies of the religious world at large on the one hand and the often spineless doctrinal positions espoused by even true believers on the other.

It must be admitted, of course, that many might throw up their hands in horror at such a development. Covenant theology to them conjures up pictures of dense tomes written by Dutchmen with equally dense names. In their opinion, it smacks of something dour, lifeless, restrictive, even oppressive. And to be fair, certain of its most formidable exponents and champions have on occasion perhaps tended to give this impression. Rightly understood, however, covenant theology provides a most important framework within which God's dealings with man can be more fully appreciated and more profoundly admired, and at the outset of this discussion it is only proper that we should consider some reasons why this should be so.[2]

First and foremost, the whole idea of a covenant between God and man is a central theme of Scripture. Our Bible is divided into two 'Testaments', a word which would be better rendered as 'Covenants'. Within its covers we find many instances of the word 'covenant', in most of which the covenant is represented as being a manifestation of divine grace and a source of comfort and confidence to God's people. God made a covenant with Noah after the flood, for example, to assure him and his descendants that he would never again destroy life in this way (Genesis 9:8-17). Later in Genesis we see God making – and renewing – a covenant with Abraham, by which God promised to Abraham seed in whom all the nations of the earth would be blessed (Genesis 12, 15, 17). Here we have a reference to the Messiah who would one day come, a Messiah who would inherit the covenant promises subsequently given to David that his throne would be an everlasting one (Psalm 89:3-4; 2 Samuel 7:12-16).

We also find references in Scripture to the 'old covenant'. This is confused in the minds of some people with the so-called 'covenant of works', which is really a theological term for the formal relationship between God and Adam before the Fall. Perhaps 'Adamic administration' would be a better term for the latter, in order to avoid such confusion.[3] The Bible rather uses the term 'old covenant' with reference to the covenant made with Israel through Moses on Sinai. This was never a covenant of works: it was established in the wake of God's gracious deliverance of Israel from Egypt, and the ceremonial law which it embraces displays with overwhelming clarity that forgiveness of sins is based on substitutionary sacrifice rather than on merit. Obedience to the law which is such a prominent feature of the 'old covenant' instituted at Sinai is to be understood in the light of the fact that the children of Israel had *already* been redeemed and were now formally bound as God's chosen people to take him as their God and to walk in all his ways.[4]

The 'old covenant' was therefore a covenant of grace. Here again, however, some element of confusion has arisen. The term 'covenant of grace' is frequently used by theologians to denote the divine plan to save sinners; others carefully distinguish the 'covenant of redemption' made between the three Persons of the Trinity from the 'covenant of grace' made between God and man. The 'covenant of redemption' and the 'covenant of grace' are most certainly biblical *concepts*, but they are not biblical *terms* as such. Rather, the Bible speaks of the 'old covenant' and the 'new covenant', the latter fulfilling and greatly excelling the former. The essence of this new covenant is that God graciously promises to be our God, and to take us to be his people. This is how Hebrews 8: 8-13 puts it, quoting Jeremiah 31: 31-34.

> Behold, the days come, saith the Lord, when I will make a new covenant with the house of Israel and with the house of Judah: not according to the covenant that I made with their fathers in the day when I took them by the hand to lead them out of the land of Egypt; because they continued not in my covenant, and I regarded them not, saith the Lord. For this is the covenant that I will make with the house of Israel after those days, saith the Lord; I will put my laws into their mind, and write them in their hearts: and I will be to them a God, and they shall be to me a people: and they shall not teach every man his neighbour, and every man his brother, saying, Know the Lord: for all shall know me, from the least to the greatest. For I will be merciful to their unrighteousness, and their sins and their iniquities will I remember no more. In that he saith, A new covenant, he hath made the first old.

According to these verses and similar declarations in Ezekiel 36:25-38 and 37:21-28, the new covenant entails priceless privileges for the Christian, none more so than a new and vital relationship with God himself. But perhaps the most wonderful thing of all is that the covenant is sealed with the blood of none other than the Son of God (Matthew 26:28; 1 Corinthians 11:25). He is the mediator of the new covenant, he is its surety, it is his blood that guarantees the privileges promised above. In him all God's promises 'are yea, and . . . Amen' (2 Corinthians 1:20). The new covenant in Christ's blood can never be undermined or overruled. 'For the mountains shall depart, and the hills be removed; but my kindness shall not depart from thee, neither shall the covenant of my peace be removed, saith the Lord that hath mercy on thee' (Isaiah 54:10). If Isaiah could speak in such terms of the old covenant, how much more comfort and encouragement can Christ's people derive from the new covenant, the manifestation *par excellence* of God's grace! In the words of John Murray, 'The covenant is the sum-total of the grace, blessing, truth, and relationship comprised in that redemption which was secured by Jesus' blood.'[5]

The whole concept of the covenant relationship between God and his people is to be found woven through the pages of Scripture, and for that basic reason it demands our attention. There are also, however, certain practical reasons which commend the covenant to us. As has already become apparent, the covenant established by the Father and guaranteed by the blood of the Son is a source of confidence, of assurance, of immense consolation. To have the God of heaven as our God, to be counted among his chosen, covenant people – the realization of these thrilling truths is enough to make the weakest Christian willing to challenge world, flesh and devil. Salvation is based on covenant promises, and as a result it is founded on a rock that cannot move. Moreover, the covenant is a direct encouragement to sanctification. Those who enjoy the privilege of being God's people are also to endeavour to conform to his image, as children to their father. Indeed, the new covenant includes an express promise that God will write his law on the hearts of his people, and that in consequence they will be willing and eager to obey his commandments (Hebrews 8:10).

Confidence and sanctification are direct results of a true

appreciation of the nature and value of God's covenant dealings with his people, but they are far from being the only consequences. Another obvious one is encouragement to, and freedom in, prayer. We can be bold to enter into God's presence because he is *our* God, and because we are *his* people. Moreover, we can pray in confidence on the basis of his covenant promises to hear us, to answer us, to aid us in our distress, to guide us in his paths, to guard us from our enemies. If we turn to the subject of evangelism, there again God's covenant is a major encouragement to his people. They are to have pity on those as yet outside the covenant. They are also to preach and teach the blessings of the covenant, implicitly if not explicitly. These blessings are none other than a new relationship with God through Christ, a new nature, an intimate knowledge of God himself, and the forgiveness of sins; but hand in hand with them go the responsibilities of the covenant, namely submitting to a new lordship and living in new obedience to God (Hebrews 8:10-11). A balanced evangelism sets forth both blessings and responsibilities: they may not be set out in specific covenantal terms, but the covenantal context is important in determining the content of the message preached.

The covenant concept deserves our attention not only because it is so obviously part of Scripture, therefore, but also because of its practical relevance to Christian living. There is, however, one other reason why we should give it more respect, and that is its importance in the history of the faith. References to the covenant may be found in the works of church fathers like Irenaeus and Augustine, but it was the Reformation that made it a vital part of Christian thinking. From the 1520s onwards, leading teachers such as Zwingli, Bullinger, Bucer and Peter Martyr were expounding the concept of the covenant. By the 1530s it was to be found in the writings of William Tyndale, and although Calvin does not discuss it specifically in his *Insti-*

tutes, it forms an important theme in his sermons. Prominent English Reformers such as John Bradford, William Perkins and Thomas Cartwright had come to appreciate the value of the covenant framework by the end of the sixteenth century, and in the next century it was adopted by virtually all the most important figures among the Puritans. The covenant constituted a key element in the Westminster Confession of Faith, the Savoy Declaration of the Congregational-Independents (1658), and the 1689 Baptist Confession, and its implications were worked out in detail by influential Continental theologians like Cocceius and Witsius.[6]

Wales did not remain isolated from these important theological developments. Indeed, it could well be argued that the covenant exerted a more lasting and a more thorough influence on theological thinking in Wales than it did in England. John Penry, the first major figure in modern Welsh Nonconformity, conceived of his salvation in covenant terms. So did Vavasor Powell, one of the leading Welsh Puritans. Griffith Jones of Llanddowror, the man who prepared the way for the Methodist Revival, called his English translation of his own commentary on the Catechism of the Church of England, *The Christian Covenant.*[7]

When we come to the Methodists themselves, we find the influence of covenant thought undeniable. It provided the grand theme for William Williams of Pantycelyn's majestic poem, *Golwg ar Deyrnas Crist* ['A View of the Kingdom of Christ']. More prosaic but no less valuable are the superb exposition of the subject in Thomas Charles's *Geiriadur Ysgrythurol* ['Scriptural Dictionary'] and the concise, precise article in the Calvinistic Methodists' Confession of Faith of 1823. A previous lecture in this series has shown the importance of the covenant in the theology of John Elias, and it was still a major force in Welsh religious thought in the middle of the last century, as reflected especially in some notable Welsh hymns.[8]

For all the biblical, practical and historical importance of God's covenant with man, however, the other side of the covenant is not without its significance. One of the distinguishing characteristics of God's covenant is that it is not an agreement between equals. It is a gracious covenant given by God, to be accepted by man. There is no haggling over terms or discussion of amendments: the covenant is the free gift of a gracious God, and to be accepted as such. At the same time, however, the whole concept of a covenant includes mutual obligations of faithfulness and devotion. Those who enjoy the privileges of God's covenant are to be constant in their loyalty and obedience to such a gracious God. Indeed, it was one of God's chief complaints against the Israelites that they neglected to keep his covenant (see, for example, Jeremiah 22:6-9; Ezekiel 16:59; Malachi 2:8-10). The mark of the true Israelite, on the other hand, was that his allegiance to his covenant God remained steadfast, that he bound himself to be faithful to the God who had entered into covenant with him. Circumcision and the observance of the ceremonial and civil laws were outward indications of such allegiance, but we also find in Scripture references to men responding to God's covenant by making specific and explicit covenants with God. It is the historical development and contemporary relevance of this practice which is of particular interest to this present discussion.

First of all, we should consider the scriptural evidence for such covenants. They may be listed as follows:

Moses and the people, Deuteronomy 26:16-19; 29:9-13

Joshua and the people, Joshua 24: 24-25

Jehoiada and the people, 2 Kings 11:17/2 Chron. 23:16

Josiah and the people, 2 Kings 23:3/2 Chron. 34:31-33

Asa and the people, 2 Chronicles 15:10-15

Hezekiah and the people, 2 Chronicles 29:10

The restored Jews, Ezra 10:3-5; Nehemiah 9:38; 10:29-31

The redeemed Israel, Jeremiah 50:4-5

The Bible also uses the word 'covenant' to refer to an agreement between two men or two parties, such as that between David and Jonathan recorded in 1 Samuel 18:3 and 23:18, but agreements of this nature are not directly relevant to our current purpose. What is relevant, and what is common to the list of covenants set out above, is that they were covenants made *with God*. Most of them were also covenants binding people together, but what distinguishes them is that these people were bound together in covenant with God himself.

One point that demands discussion here is the fundamental nature of these covenants with God. Both old and new covenants are clearly and unmistakably gracious in essence. Man can never merit these tokens of God's mercy; all that he can do is to accept them – accept them humbly, gratefully, eagerly. The question that arises, however, is as follows: is the making of a covenant with God an attempt to win God's favour, an endeavouring to persuade God to accept us on the basis of our consecration and faithfulness? In other words, is the making of a covenant with God in effect a variation on the theme of justification by works?

A glance at the covenants listed in the Bible dispels this fear instantly. In each case the covenant with God is a formal acknowledgement of, and response to, God's gracious covenant with his people. It is a hearty response, a thankful response, a response which takes the form of wholehearted consecration to the God who has remembered them in mercy. Every item in the above list is to be understood in the light of the fact that God had *already* made a covenant with his people Israel, namely the old covenant of Sinai. What these biblical heroes did was to bind themselves to be faithful to this gracious covenant. In some cases it is obvious that they were conscious how far they themselves or their predecessors had abused or neglected this covenant. But the key element in the whole transaction is that they henceforth undertook to *be* the people of God, to be earnestly and practically what they already were in the sight of God. Their sincere desire as God's people was, in the words of Nehemiah 10:29, to 'walk in God's law . . . and to observe and do all the commandments of the LORD our Lord, and his judgments and his statutes.'

In modern times certain individual Christians and some sections of the Christian church have been stirred up by these biblical covenants to enter into similar pacts with God. These pacts have normally taken two forms. In the first place, there are many examples of covenants made by individual Christians. Living as we do in an age of shallow spirituality, these covenants might open our eyes to the earnestness, the sobriety, the gravity, the wholeheartedness, with which our forefathers viewed their God, their faith, and the eternal welfare of their souls. Secondly, we find instances of church covenants, binding church members to one another and to God, and setting forth the responsibilities of Christians in the local fellowship of the saints. These documents have a certain historical interest, but their value is not limited to the past. As more and more independent evangelical churches are being formed, and as they seek a basis on which they can organize themselves, the church covenants of a former day might well be a source of guidance even where it is felt that the practice of covenanting as such cannot be adopted.

It is these two forms of the historical covenant – those made by individuals and those made by churches – that will be discussed in the remainder of this study.

THE PERSONAL COVENANT

It seems likely that the making of personal covenants on a significant scale was really the product of the Reformation.[9] By the seventeenth century they begin to multiply, and during the eighteenth century they were a common feature of devotional life. In the nature of the case, of course, the personal covenant was a private document whose existence was usually known only to the writer, and it is therefore difficult to make precise statements about such documents as a general body of literature. It appears, however, that the practice declined during the second half of the nineteenth century, and it is perhaps no coincidence that this same period witnessed the beginning of the doctrinal, devotional and practical down-grade which was subsequently to blight Christianity.

The personal covenant usually served as a spiritual milestone, three of which deserve special attention. First of all, there was conversion. Less than a month after his conversion, C. H. Spurgeon (1834-92) made the following covenant:

> O great and unsearchable God, who knowest my heart, and triest all my ways; with a humble dependence upon the support of Thy Holy Spirit, I yield up myself to Thee; as Thy own reasonable sacrifice, I return to Thee Thine own. I would be for ever, unreservedly, perpetually Thine; whilst I am on earth, I would serve Thee; and may I enjoy Thee and praise Thee for ever! Amen.
>
> Feb. 1, 1850. CHARLES HADDON SPURGEON[10]

Indeed, it could be argued that entering into a covenant with God lies at the heart of conversion. In the words of Matthew Henry (1662-1714):

> There is true conversion where there have been covenant transactions between God and the soul. And I found that there have been such between God and my soul, and I hope in truth and righteousness. If I never did this before, I do it now; for I take God in Christ to be mine. I give up myself to be his in the bond of an everlasting covenant never-to-be-forgotten.[11]

It should be added immediately that Matthew Henry is talking here not of a *written* covenant. Making conversion dependent on a written covenant is to do away with the finished work of Christ and to substitute for it something of our own; nothing could be further from the great Welsh commentator's meaning. Nevertheless, taking God henceforth to be our God and submitting to be one of his people lies at the heart of conversion, whether it is stated explicitly in covenant terms or only implicitly as part of the whole conversion experience.[12] We find evidence of this implicit statement in the spiritual history of Howel Harris (1714-73). Writing of the time immediately prior to that Whit-Sunday in 1735 when he received assurance of the forgiveness of his sins, he says:

> I felt a strong impression on my mind to give myself to God as I was, and to leave all to follow Him. But presently I felt a strong opposition to it, backed with reasons that if I would give myself to the Lord I should lose my liberty, and would then be not my own, or in my own power; but after a great conflict for some time I was made willing to bid adieu to all things temporal, and choose the Lord for my portion.[13]

While not actually using the term 'covenant', Harris's words are steeped in covenant thought. Just over three weeks after his Whit-Sunday experience, he found his heart again melting within him with love to God:

> There was a cry in my inmost soul which I was totally unacquainted with before, 'Abba, Father! Abba, Father!' I could not help calling God my Father; I *knew* that I was His child, and that He loved me and heard me. My soul being filled and satiated, cried, 'It is enough; I am satisfied. Give me strength, and I will follow Thee through fire and water.[14]

Again the term 'covenant' is missing, but again the covenant concept is plain: the awareness of being one of God's people, the privileges which this new relationship entails, the willingness to yield himself up to God, come what may. And these elements are part and parcel of true conversion. The work of the gospel has suffered too long from a tendency to divorce faith in Christ from submission to Christ: to take Christ as Saviour without at the same time taking him also as Lord. It may be the case that in a particular individual's experience one element will loom larger and be more immediately relevant than the other; but there is no true conversion where Christ is not received both as Saviour and Lord. And wherever Christ is received as such, the covenant element is present – whether explicit or implicit, whether the new believer is consciously aware of it or not.

Sometimes, of course, it is only in looking back that one is truly aware of the nature of conversion, of what actually happened in coming to faith in Christ. This looking back might in itself lead a person either to renew his initial covenant with God or to express his gratitude and consecration in written form for the first time. On 12 January 1723, Jonathan Edwards (1703-58) came to Christ, and in that initial consecration of his life to his new Saviour and Lord he wrote out a covenant. He subsequently vowed to remember regularly this yielding of himself, and his diary testifies to such remembrance on later anniversaries of his conversion.[15] We have no evidence that Thomas Charles of Bala (1755-1814) wrote out a covenant immediately after his conversion, but on 20 January 1782, exactly nine years after that turning-point in his life, the memory of it prompted him to make the following covenantal declarations:

> This day I have been receiving from God the seal of the covenant at the sacrament. I was in the morning at the table very insensible and unaffected. But in the evening I had a most comfortable meditation on the gracious covenant which God hath made with Christ on behalf of his people. Its freeness, stability and richness are full of consolation when viewed by faith. I found myself willing and desirous above all things to receive Christ and all his fulness, as my Saviour, Lord and Master. And there is nothing my heart so much longs after as to be entirely his in time and eternity, to live and die for and to him, to glorify him with my soul and body, talents, time and possessions, with all I am and all I have.[16]

It was to mark their spiritual birthday that Jonathan Edwards and Thomas Charles made their covenants. The second obvious occasion for making a covenant was the occurrence of natural birthdays, and the opportunities which these presented for sober reflection, prayerful anticipation and a renewing of loyalty to the Lord. It was the regular practice of Thomas Richard of Fishguard (1783-1856), the formidable Methodist preacher who believed passionately in the value of personal covenanting, to renew his covenant on such occasions. For similar reasons, covenanting at New Year was popular. Thomas Richard was wont to renew his covenant at these times also; so too was David Peter (1765-1837), the influential (and evangelical) head of the Presbyterian Academy at Carmarthen from 1795 to 1835.[17] To this day the Wesleyan Methodists hold a special covenant service around the turn of the year. When undertaken properly and sincerely, there is obviously much more to this practice than the making of short-lived New Year resolutions: it is done solemnly in the presence of God, taking God as witness to the transaction and binding the covenanter to fulfil his obligations. This solemn element is apparent in the covenants of Matthew Henry, who regularly celebrated both New Year and his birthday in this manner:

> This new-year's day [*circa* 1700] I have solemnly renewed the resignation and surrender of my whole self to God, as my God, deliberately, and upon good considerations. I have renounced the world and the flesh as knowing they cannot make me happy; and have devoted my whole self to the blessed Spirit, to be enlightened, and sanctified, and so recommended to the Son, as qualified for an interest in his mediation, according to the tenor of the gospel. I likewise devote myself, through the Spirit, to the Lord Jesus Christ, as my Advocate with the Father, and my way to him; by him to be recommended to the grace and favour of God the Father, relying upon Christ's righteousness alone; for, without him, I am less than nothing, worse than nothing. I likewise devote myself, through the Lord Jesus Christ, to God the Father, as my chief good and highest end; as the author of my being, to whom I am obliged in duty; and the felicity of my being, to whom I am obliged in interest. O Lord, truly I am thy servant. I am thy servant; may I ever be free in thy service, and never desire to be free from it. Nail my ear to thy door-posts, and let me serve thee for ever.[18]

The third major factor encouraging the making of a covenant was the occurrence of an event of special personal significance. Thomas Charles was no doubt neither the first nor the last of God's people to make a special covenant at his ordination:

> May 21, 1780. I was this morning ordained Priest, – when I most solemnly and with my whole heart devoted myself with all I have to the service of God. Time, talents and all, I hope, I have been enabled to lay down at his feet: nor would I, on the most serious consideration and in my most deliberate moments, wish to retract one word I have spoken. I hope I can say that the constant and rooted desire of my soul is after God and his service.

Lewis Edwards of Bala (1809-87), who married the granddaughter of Thomas Charles and became one of the dominant figures of Welsh life in the mid-nineteenth century, composed a covenant in similar circumstances:

> And if I should have the privilege of commencing in the work of the ministry, it is on thy strength and thy enabling, great Lord, that I shall confidently rely in the face of the mighty strongholds of the devil. Let me not, gracious Father, Oh let me not rush rashly into this great and holy work without my being sent from above . . . Use me as an instrument in thy service . . . With sincere and humble confidence in thy help, O Lord, to perform this solemn covenant I now sign it on the eleventh day of February, the year of our Lord one thousand, eight hundred, and twenty-seven.[19]

Another event of special personal significance was baptism, and this was frequently regarded as a covenantal act. This was certainly how Thomas Charles regarded it, and his opinions were echoed by George Lewis of Llanuwchllyn near Bala (1763-1822). David Brainerd (1718-47) reminded his Indian converts of their baptismal pledges in an endeavour to stir them up to greater holiness of life.[20] Philip Henry (1631-96) used to gather his children together to repeat their baptismal covenant every Sunday evening :

> I take God the Father to be my chiefest good, and highest end.
>
> I take God the Son to be my Prince and Saviour.
>
> I take God the Holy Ghost to be my Sanctifier, Teacher, Guide, and Comforter.
>
> I take the word of God to be my rule in all my actions.
>
> And the people of God to be my people in all conditions.
>
> I do likewise devote and dedicate unto the Lord, my whole self, all I am, all I have, and all I can do.
>
> And this I do deliberately, sincerely, freely, and for ever.

When the children grew up they each wrote out this covenant in full and set their names to it. Their father then kept the documents, warning his children that these would be produced in evidence against them were they ever to depart from the ways of the Lord. Henry regarded the partaking of the Lord's Supper as an indication of the children's consciously taking the covenant for themselves and making their own personal act of self-dedication to the Lord.[21]

Other important events or circumstances, such as a new situation in life, or the contemplation of an unknown future, could also prove a stimulus to the making of a covenant. Before William Carey (1761-1834) set out for India, he bound John Ryland, John Sutcliff, Andrew Fuller and Samuel Pearce in a covenant that 'they should never cease till death to stand by him'. Carey viewed this covenant as a stout rope held fast by the others and attached to himself as he ventured into the depths of an unexplored and potentially dangerous pit. Having arrived in India he drew up another covenant which he and his companions there were to read three times a year in each mission station in order to encourage perseverance in their great work. In the case of John Fletcher of Madeley (1729-85), first president of the Countess of Huntingdon's theological college at Trefeca, we read that on his wedding-day on 12 November 1781 he and his new wife sang Charles Wesley's covenant hymn and then joined in perpetual covenant together to the Lord.[22]

New light from Scripture, new tokens of God's love, new evidences of his providential mercies might serve as further stimuli, in much the same way as Old Testament patriarchs set up altars to mark gracious visitations of their God. Howel Harris so longed to have the company and fellowship of a like-minded and like-spirited man in his native Breconshire that when Howel Davies (*c.*1716-70), the local schoolmaster, was converted through Harris's ministry the two resolved to enter into a written covenant, joining together 'in the dedication of self to Christ'. No doubt Harris considered himself as privileged as Bunyan's Christian when, after the martyrdom of Faithful, Hopeful 'joined himself unto him, and entring into a brotherly covenant, told him that he would be his companion'.[23]

Perhaps the best-known example from Wales, however, is that of the eloquent Baptist, Christmas Evans (1766-1838), who wrote a number of full and rich covenants at crucial stages of his spiritual pilgrimage. One was written as a direct result of his deliverance from the coldly intellectual clutches of Sandemanianism. Another marked his departure from Anglesey, after a fruitful ministry there, to set out for the relatively unfamiliar county of Glamorgan; and when he was guided to move within the latter county, from Caerphilly to Cardiff, he made yet another covenant.[24]

Less familiar, but overflowing with genuine spiritual pathos, is the covenant of William Williams (1732-99), the founder of the Baptist cause in Cardigan. It was written out when he was but twenty-one years old, to mark the death of his young wife. Having listed his covenant pledges, he closes with the following declaration:

> On the Sabbath day, December 30, 1753, after serious consideration, I came to the happy decision, that whatever others might do, I shall serve the Lord, Joshua 24:15.
>
> WILLIAM WILLIAMS[25]

* * * * *

Some of the reasons for these personal covenants have already been touched on. In general terms, they were the grateful response of serious-minded Christians to the grace of God manifested in his covenant with them. Whether it was to mark conversion, significant dates or special providences, this grateful response allied to consecration – initial or renewed – lay at the bottom of the covenants. In this sense they make heart-warming reading: the spirit of sincere devotion throbs through every pledge. No Christian can fail to be moved – and challenged – by the genuine desires recorded to serve God both solemnly and wholeheartedly. Indeed, as already observed, every true Christian has in effect made a similar response and should be activated by similar desires.

Where Christians might differ, however, is over the value of *written* covenants. In his heart every Christian has entered into covenant with God – has taken him for his God, has engaged to serve this God all his days, has promised to cleave to him in life and in death. While these pledges do not make a person a Christian, he nevertheless cannot be a Christian without them. But a person can certainly be a Christian without setting out his covenantal engagement in written form.

In favour of the written covenant there are a number of arguments. Philip Doddridge (1702-51) notes them as follows in his *Rise and Progress of Religion in the Soul* (1744):

> Such solemnity in the manner of doing it, is certainly very reasonable in the nature of things; and sure it is highly expedient, for binding to the Lord such a treacherous heart, as we know our own to be. It will be pleasant to reflect upon it, as done at such and such a time, with such and such circumstances of place and method, which may serve to strike the memory and the conscience. The sense of the vows of GOD which are upon you will strengthen you in an hour of temptation; and the recollection may also encourage your humble boldness and freedom in applying to Him, under the character and relation of your covenant GOD and Father, as future exigencies may require.[26]

At bottom, Doddridge believed that formal written covenants were of major assistance in sealing and confirming a sinner's conversion. In this respect he followed the teaching of Joseph Alleine (1634-68), the ardent evangelist who was burdened with the spiritual needs of Wales and whose *Alarm to the Unconverted* was first published in Welsh in 1693.[27] Indeed, both Doddridge and Alleine provide examples of covenants which a repentant sinner could adopt for himself.

It must be emphasized here, however, that neither Alleine nor Doddridge believed that a verbal or written covenant was *essential* to salvation. William Guthrie (1620-69), one of the gospel's shining lights in western Scotland during the mid-seventeenth century, drew the distinction carefully as follows:

> I grant this express covenanting and transacting with God is not absolutely necessary for a man's salvation; for if any person close heartily and sincerely with God, offering Himself in Christ in the gospel, his soul and state are thereby secured, according to the Scripture, although he utter not words with his mouth; but this express verbal covenanting with God is very expedient, for the better wellbeing of a man's state, and for his more comfortable maintaining of an interest in Christ Jesus.[28]

It was this element of formality which was so important in the eyes of such men as Doddridge, Alleine and Guthrie. In the heat of the moment sinners might 'decide for Christ' without truly understanding the nature of such a decision. What the written covenant provided was a means whereby the mind, the heart and the will could be engaged together in formally declaring allegiance to God. Formality in religion is often equated with lifelessness and lukewarmness, but these Christians were far from being formal in that sense. Rather did they consider the formal element in the covenant to be a decided advantage: it nailed the sinner down, it made him consider seriously what he was about, it bound him to his God in a manner which could not lightly be overthrown. And were it to be overthrown or laid aside, the consequences would have to be faced.

So convinced of the importance of this formal element was Michael Roberts (1780-1849), the Methodist preacher from Pwllheli and friend of John Elias, that he treated it almost as a legal document. Having listed fourteen items in which he covenanted with God, he signed the document, attached tape to it, secured it with a large seal of red wax and wrote his name again below the seal. Moreover, he vowed to read and meditate on his covenant frequently, and bound himself by oath to keep the covenant pledges conscientiously. Samuel Pearce (1766-99), friend and ardent supporter of William Carey, went still further. Almost certainly influenced by Doddridge's arguments in favour of a solemn and formal covenant, Pearce listed his pledges and then sealed them by signing the document in his own blood.[29]

The sealing virtues of a written covenant were not the only advantages which it afforded. As we have already seen, meditation on the covenant and its frequent renewal could be of decided spiritual benefit, spurring the believer on to more dedicated service. Renewal of the covenant should not be understood in terms of the Keswick teaching concerning 'full surrender'. The true Christian makes a 'full surrender' of himself to Christ at his conversion, taking Christ as his Saviour and Lord. What the written covenant provided was a record of that self-dedication and a means whereby the Christian could subsequently monitor his spiritual progress. Renewal of the covenant would then be particularly appropriate after a period of spiritual coldness or lethargy, or again in grateful response to some new manifestation of God's grace. 'Covenants renewed in these particulars', declared Philip Henry on New Year's Day 1665:

> 1. by the Lord's help and purpose to be more substantial in secret worship. 2. more sparing of precious time. 3. more constant in reading the Scriptures alone and meditating in them. 4. more careful to improve all opportunities of doing good to souls . . . 5. less fearful about events, when in a way of duty, in all which I have lately missed it, but the Lord has pardoned me in Christ Jesus.[30]

These were not the only occasions when the covenant might be renewed. In William Guthrie's opinion, meditation on the covenant was of special value in the face of pressing problems and apparently insurmountable difficulties. In such circumstances it could prove a direct stimulus to courage, confidence and perseverance. Similarly, times when God appeared afar off and insensitive to urgent needs could be endured more comfortably by recourse to the covenant and the formal pledges contained therein, 'for richer, for poorer; for better, for worse'.[31]

The covenant might supply a more regular basis for self-examination and a spur to reconsecration before approaching the communion table. In observing the Lord's Supper at Kidderminster, for example, Richard Baxter (1615-91) would lead his congregation in covenant renewal. And lest anyone should eat the bread and drink the cup unworthily, the covenant could also serve as a check to sinful tendencies. In Michael Roberts's words:

> And if it happens that I shall deny the faith in opinion or practice, I shall be guilty not only of sinning against those parts of the Bible, but also of breaking my covenant with God, and of drawing back to perdition. O! O! may God preserve me![32]

Awareness of broken pledges could be a powerful factor in the still more solemn dedication of oneself in a renewed covenant. More positively, renewal might be the result of heartfelt gratitude for gracious providences. Spurgeon supplies the following exhortation:

> There are many occasions in our experience when we may very rightly, and with benefit, renew our covenant with God. After *recovery from sickness* when, like Hezekiah, we have had a new term of years added to our life, we may fitly do it. After any *deliverance from trouble*, when our joys bud forth anew, let us again visit the foot of the cross, and renew our consecration. Especially, let us do this after any *sin which has grieved the*

Holy Spirit, or brought dishonour upon the cause of God; let us then look to that blood which can make us whiter than snow, and again offer ourselves unto the Lord. We should not only let our troubles confirm our dedication to God, but *our prosperity* should do the same. If we ever meet with occasions which deserve to be called 'crowning mercies,' then, surely, if He hath crowned *us,* we ought also to crown our God; let us bring forth anew all the jewels of the divine regalia which have been stored in the jewel-closet of our heart, and let our God sit upon the throne of our love, arrayed in royal apparel. If we would learn to profit by our prosperity, we should not need so much adversity. If we would gather from a kiss all the good it might confer upon us, we should not so often smart under the rod. Have we lately received some blessing which we little expected? Has the Lord put our feet in a large room? Can we sing of mercies multiplied? Then this is the day to put our hand upon the horns of the altar, and say, 'Bind me here, my God; bind me here with cords, even for ever.' Inasmuch as we need the fulfilment of new promises from God, let us offer renewed prayers that our old vows may not be dishonoured. Let us this morning make with him a sure covenant, because of the pains of Jesus.[33]

* * * * *

Despite the obvious advantages of a written covenant and all the above testimonies to its spiritual value, it must nevertheless be acknowledged that the practice was far from being adopted by all Christians in the past and that it has to all intents and purposes disappeared by today. It must also be acknowledged that there are certain genuine reasons for the decline of the practice. Most important of all from the standpoint of the true Christian was the obvious danger of legalism. In his *Human Nature in its Fourfold*

State, Thomas Boston (1676-1732) notes that it is quite possible for a man to enter into a legal covenant with God rather than trust in Christ with the whole heart.[34] The result is that such a man believes that it is his consecration, his dedication of himself, that saves him, rather than the Son of God. In other words, a covenant could be represented as a 'good work' and might undermine the cardinal doctrine of justification by faith in Christ.

John Brown of Haddington (1722-87) records that Alleine's directions concerning the making of a covenant proved a serious stumbling-block to his coming to faith in Christ. He consecrated his life to God without first trusting in the righteousness of Christ, and consequently was guilty of 'putting my fashion of religion in Christ's room, setting up my formal prayers, etc., for my Saviour, yea, for my God'. (It should be added, nevertheless, that this experience did not prevent Brown from making a covenant with God much later, *after* he had come to trust in Christ.)[35] It was in all probability this danger which led J. C. Ryle to add the following rider in publishing the covenant of the leading Yorkshire Methodist, William Grimshaw (1708-63):

> In giving this covenant to my readers, I would carefully abstain from saying that such covenants ought always to be made, or to be pressed on all Christians. So far from that, I think them likely to do harm to some minds. Let every one use his liberty. He that finds it good to make a covenant, let him make it. But let him not condemn his neighbour who makes none.[36]

A second peril was that a written covenant might become a source of spiritual complacency even in those who had truly believed in Christ. The covenant could indeed spur on believers or remind them of how far they had strayed from their initial profession; but in other cases it might serve to persuade a believer that all was well between him and God, that a formal transaction had been entered into and that his spiritual welfare was thereby guaranteed. This was, of course, one of the fundamental errors of the Jews. They assumed that their physical lineage, God's dealings with the nation in the past, and the possession of the law, set them apart as the special objects of God's favour, and that nothing more was required of them.

Even in our days there is always a temptation for a true believer to look back upon his conversion and to recount the circumstances of his initial trusting in Christ rather than undertake an assessment of his present spiritual condition. A written covenant might well add extra force to such a temptation, encouraging a religion essentially static and lifeless, a religion which lives in the past and feeds upon the experiences of yesterday.

The two-fold dangers of legalism and complacency might pose serious obstacles to the uninstructed and the weak-minded. They certainly constitute genuine reasons why the practice of covenanting should be undertaken only with the greatest care and forethought, and partly explain why it was never adopted by all God's people.

There was, however, another danger which might deter some from entering into formal covenant with God. Those Christians with sensitive consciences might recoil from anything that smacked of bargaining with God. There is indeed a suspicion in some covenants that the writers go beyond the proper limits of holy boldness and put unseemly and unwarranted pressure on God. Perhaps this is why Thomas Richard of Fishguard included the following apology in one of his covenants:

> O, what is miserable man to enter into covenant with the Great God! O that my Lord would not be angry with me for venturing upon this once again, for it is

according to thy word, according to the custom of thy people Israel, as with Abraham and all his spiritual descendants in possession of the same faith to the end of the world; therefore I too, the most miserable of all, once again at the end of my life shall take the Lord to be my God, to walk in his ways, and to keep his statutes and his commandments and his judgements, and to give heed to his voice . . . Thou dost say, 'Come now, and let us reason together: incline your ear, and come unto me: hear, and your soul shall live; and I will make an everlasting covenant with you, even the sure mercies of David.' These words show that making a covenant with the Lord is in accordance with the word of the Lord, which demonstrates his approval, so that those things that Amen says may indeed be said; and because the infinite God who has taken the Amen upon himself and given his infinite self to be an Amen to this, I at his feet do declare and witness and sign with my own hand, the 12th of February, 1850, this covenant, Amen. Amen. Amen.[37]

In the attitude of Thomas Richard we see combined holy boldness and godly humility, but in other hands the covenant might encourage the idea that one could strike an agreement with God to one's own advantage. In systematized form, this was in effect Arminianism, and perhaps the use of the covenant or pledge by Arminian evangelists during the last century cast some shadow of doubt over its worth among those who clung to the old paths. Charles Finney (1792-1875), the pioneer of modern Arminian evangelism, sought to persuade his hearers to commit themselves publicly to Christ by taking a pledge, and the pledge was later formalized by Edward Payson Hammond (1831-1910) in the shape of a 'covenant card', the forerunner of the 'decision card' which was to occupy such a prominent place in evangelistic methods.[38] The following example of a decision card is derived from the 1859 Revival in Ireland:

MY COVENANT

I take God the Father to be my God (1 Thess. 1:9)
I take Christ the Son to be my Saviour (Acts 5:31)
I take the Holy Spirit to be my Sanctifier (1 Peter 1:2)
I take the Word of God to be my Rule (2 Tim. 3:16)
I take the people of God to be my people (Ruth 1:16,17)
I dedicate my whole self to the Lord (Romans 14:7,8)
and I do this deliberately (Joshua 24:15)
and sincerely (2 Cor. 1:12)
and freely (Psalm 110:3)
and for ever (Romans 8:35-39)[39]

While this form of decision card was not altogether unrelated to the model covenants provided by Alleine and Doddridge, the theology behind its use was wholly different. In the latter case the covenant merely sealed a transaction that had already taken place, a transaction which laid the emphasis on God's gracious covenant dealings with man. On the other hand, the use of the decision card, often accompanied by the temperance pledge, was usually based on the belief that man had the ability to choose Christ, and that all he needed to do so was some effective prodding. It would seem that as the new evangelistic theology gained ground in the second half of the nineteenth century, so the appreciation of God's covenant declined and with it the traditional response to that covenant.

There is, however, a still more basic factor responsible for the decline of the practice during the last hundred years or so, namely the general decay of experimental religion over that period. The theological downgrade can be traced easily enough; but hand-in-hand with the departure from orthodoxy went a devotional decline, a gradual lowering of spiritual standards even among the Lord's people.

More particularly, the solemn, serious, careful, responsible elements of the Christian faith have been increasingly at a premium, and the desire for superficial spiritual thrills, for the glossy and the gimmicky, has correspondingly increased. The friends of Vavasor Powell (1617-70) wrote that he

> was a faithful and diligent observer of the outgoings of God upon his soul, whereof he kept a daily account and record, taking notice both of the actings of grace, and the stirrings of corruption, and the assaults of sin and Satan, or world made upon him.[40]

In this day and age, such records – diaries, spiritual autobiographies, personal confessions of faith, covenants – are conspicuous by their absence.

There is, of course, no biblical injunction that every Christian must make a written covenant with God. It cannot be denied, however, that *every* Christian has entered into covenant – written or otherwise – by taking God in Christ to be his God, by acknowledging himself to be among God's people. All that a written covenant does is to make the covenant engagement more regular, more explicit, more specific. If it proves an aid to a more serious profession, a more watchful life, a more tender conscience towards God, it will have served a most important purpose. It would be well for us all if we could echo Thomas Charles's words on the first day of 1779:

> I most cheerfully and sincerely surrender myself and all thou hast bestowed upon me, (for I have nothing else that is good) to thee and thy service this new year and forevermore. Behold, I am thy servant: help me to serve and glorify thee. I am thine; keep me. I am thine; never leave me. May I never be permitted to dishonour thy dear name.[41]

THE CHURCH COVENANT

In turning to the church covenant, it might be helpful to note that there are in reality two aspects to this subject, one of general interest to all groups of Christians and the other of particular importance to those assemblies or individuals who are concerned with the nature of the gathered church. The first might be termed 'covenanting as Christians', the second 'covenanting as a church'.

It is this second aspect which will be of primary concern in this chapter, but even where the formal idea of a 'church covenant' is not adopted, the practice of covenanting together as a group of Christians deserves careful consideration in its own right. Its basic justification is that it is eminently scriptural. All the Old Testament covenants with God listed earlier have the same essential characteristics: a solemn leaguing together before God to seek him and to walk in all his ways. Their significance and relevance are reinforced by New Testament passages to which tremendous promises are attached: 'Again I say unto you, That if two of you shall agree on earth as touching any thing that they shall ask, it shall be done for them of my Father which is in heaven' (Matthew 18: 19).

Covenants of this kind have been a feature of Christian living down the centuries. By their very nature, however, it is not easy to come across documents giving details of the actual agreements. These were covenants of a more informal character in that they were not necessarily associated directly with churches as institutions and are therefore not always recorded in official papers. One instance is the agreeing together to lead consecrated lives, something which was to be a feature of pledges in certain specific church covenants. An early example is found in a letter from Pliny the Younger to the Emperor Trajan, written about AD 112, in which he states that Christians in his area 'bind themselves by an oath, not for the commission of any crime, but to abstain from theft, robbery, adultery and breach of faith, and not to deny a deposit when it was claimed'.[42]

Another example is the agreeing together to pray for revival. Griffith Jones of Llanddowror (1683-1761) proposed a plan to this end in the mid-1730s: 'Besides the general regard which God has to the prayers of his people', he argued, 'he gives particular encouragement to believe that they shall speed better, when they unite and agree on some special errand and request to carry before him.' It was hardly a coincidence, then, that at the very time that Griffith Jones and his friends were uniting in prayer God was working a spiritual transformation in the lives of a certain Howel Harris in Breconshire and a certain Daniel Rowland in Cardiganshire. The practice was not restricted to the eighteenth century. The Beddgelert Revival of 1817-22 was preceded by an agreement whereby church members undertook to set aside a specific part of each day to pray for a divine visitation.[43]

One other prayer concert of still greater significance should not be omitted. In 1748 Jonathan Edwards issued his *Humble Attempt to Promote Explicit Agreement and Visible Union of God's People . . . in Extraordinary Prayer for the Revival of Religion and the Advancement of Christ's Kingdom on Earth.* Apart from its immediate impact on America, England and Scotland, it was to have more far-reaching consequences. In 1784 John Sutcliff of Olney (1752-1814) was so moved in reading it that he proposed to the Northamptonshire Association of Particular Baptists that the churches should set apart the first Monday of every month for prayer for revival. In recommending this proposal to the churches, the Northamptonshire Association's circular letter encouraged them to pray not only for revival but also for 'the spread of the Gospel to the most distant parts of the habitable globe'. The outcome was the founding of the Particular Baptist Society for the Propagation of the Gospel among the Heathen, the sending of William Carey to India, and the beginning of the modern missionary movement.[44]

Although the underlying theological premises were very different, agreements to pray together for a visitation of the Holy Spirit were further promoted by Charles Finney's rules for producing revivals. The wisdom of adopting rules for producing revivals may properly be questioned, but there can be little doubt that Finney's instructions were widely received and acted upon. His *Lectures* were published in Welsh in 1839, and from that time onwards there are increasing reports of prayer meetings being held specifically to pray for revival. Sometimes these were organized on a denominational basis. The first day of 1840, for example, was set apart by the Independent churches of Caernarvonshire as a day of prayer for a religious awakening. Monmouthshire Baptists and South Wales Independents spent 1 August 1858 in prayer for a more extensive outpouring of the Holy Spirit, and the North Wales Association of the Calvinistic Methodists set apart the entire second week of January 1860 in thanksgiving for the awakening already apparent and to pray for a still greater manifestation of the Spirit's work.[45]

More common by far, however, were the prayer meetings organized at a local level in which Christians promised to pray specifically for revival. One example was the promise made by some young Welsh ministers to hold whole-day prayer meetings once a month from 1903 onwards. Another was the pledge undertaken by a small band of Christians at a meeting convened by Dr Martyn Lloyd-Jones at Sandfields, Aberafan, in 1930 to 'wait upon

God for one half-hour daily, in particular prayer for, (i) A revival of religion (ii) For one another'.[46]

While these agreements admittedly consisted more of promises than of specific detailed covenants, their significance within the whole range of covenantal undertakings should not be ignored. In other cases the covenant element was more pronounced. It was not uncommon for Christians in English parish churches during the second half of the sixteenth century, before the general spread of Separatist ideas, to covenant together 'to follow after the Lord in the purity of his worship' or to keep themselves from known evils. In other words, the godly members of the congregation were bound together in covenant while remaining faithful members of the Anglican Church. There is even one instance of a covenant drawn up in the parish of Worksop in 1607 to counteract the ideas of John Smyth (*c.* 1554-1612), an ardent proponent of the Separatist church covenant.[47]

In the case of the Methodist Church, the annual covenant service is designed not to constitute the church but to encourage members, in the words of Charles Wesley's covenant hymn, to

> Give up ourselves, through Jesu's power,
> His name to glorify;
> And promise, in this sacred hour,
> For God to live and die.

This is surely the essence of the Christian life, and the scriptural precedents for making such covenants encourage us to believe that they could be adopted on a far wider scale than is perhaps the case at present.

* * * * *

The second aspect of the church covenant, the covenanting together as a church, is nevertheless of perhaps greater historical and ecclesiastical interest. The idea possibly originated with the German Anabaptists; at least, it was to be found in their writings from the 1520s onwards.[48] The Reformation at Geneva took place in a covenantal context, one example being the opportunity for the whole city to pledge its loyalty to the confession of faith drawn up by Calvin and Farel in 1536, which was to all intents and purposes a religious and social compact.[49] By the mid-sixteenth century it had been adopted in Scotland, but there it took the form first of district covenants and later of national covenants which were ultimately to reject the concept of separate congregational covenants. Elsewhere, however, the last-named were becoming more popular, and during the reign of the Catholic Queen Mary (1553-58), a number of former Anglican congregations who fled to the Continent made use of the covenant idea in establishing churches there.[50]

The first record of a church covenant in Britain is to be found in the writings of an anonymous Separatist in the early 1570s. It began with the declaration that 'I have joined myself to the church of Christ wherein I have yielded myself subject to the discipline of God's word as I promised at my baptism.' According to Archbishop Parker (1504-75), an avowed opponent of the Separatists, 'To this protestation the congregation singularly did swear, and after took the communion for ratification of their assent.'

It is possible that this covenant belonged to the congregation of Richard Fitz in London, the earliest Separatist church in Britain of which any considerable historical record has been preserved.[51] What is certain is that the well-known Separatist congregation established at Norwich by Robert Browne (*c.* 1550-1633) around 1580/1 was founded on the basis of a specific covenant, and later Separatists seem to have adopted the idea generally. John Greenwood's congregation in London, formed in the late 1580s, had one; so did John Smyth's church at Gainsborough in 1605/6 and that established by Henry Jacob (1563-1624) at Southwark, London, in 1616.[52]

The persistence of the last-named church and its contribution through Henry Jessey (1601-63), a subsequent pastor, to the founding of the first gathered congregation in Wales at Llanfaches in 1639, adds a particular significance to its original covenant of 1616. At the end of a day of fasting, prayer, and consideration of the organization of the congregation, those who wished to associate themselves with the church

> joining together joined both hands each with [an]other brother and stood in a ringwise: their intent being declared, H. Jacob and each of the rest made some confession or profession of their faith and repentance, some were longer some were briefer, then they covenanted together to walk in all God's ways as he had revealed or should make known to them.[53]

It seems to have been common practice for Independent churches established later in the seventeenth century to have a covenant basis. Many Baptist congregations also had covenants, although there was a certain reluctance to adopt the practice wholesale for reasons which will be discussed later.[54]

The most widespread implementation of the covenant idea, however, was to be found in New England. The Pilgrim Fathers took to America the covenant originally drawn up at the founding of the church at Gainsborough-Scrooby, Lincolnshire, and employed it in the 'Mayflower Church' in Plymouth Colony. In fact, the 'Mayflower' colonists virtually created a civil state on the basis of a formal covenant, and later settlers in New England extended this practice.[55] The result was a social system founded essentially on the church covenant. At the heart of each town was the church, and at the heart of each church was the covenant. Those who were members of the church by virtue of engaging in covenant were also, in Massachusetts and New Haven at least, the only inhabitants who had the right to vote in civil affairs. Other inhabitants were expected to attend the church and to pay taxes for the support of the minister, but were excluded from a full role in the life of the community. As a result the covenant assumed widespread importance, not only in the ecclesiastical sphere but also in the development of New England as a whole.[56]

The church covenant never had such social implications in Wales, but its significance in the growth of Dissenting congregations should not be ignored. The first Welshman known to have entered into church covenant was John Penry (1563-93). He himself was fully aware of the covenant basis of the church, with which 'I do believe that the Lord God of his mere favour hath entered into covenant that he will be their God and that they shall be his people'. No less significant was the fact that in 1592 he joined the Separatist church of Greenwood and Barrow in London, which was organized on strictly covenant terms.[57]

Penry's immediate influence on his native country was limited, however, and not until 1639 was the first gathered church established in Wales. Although there is no documentary evidence extant, it seems certain that this church, at Llanfaches in Gwent, was formed on the basis of a covenant. William Wroth (1576-1641) was the pastor, but the church was founded with the help of Henry Jessey, the pastor of the covenant-based church established by Henry Jacob at Southwark. It was through the efforts of Wroth and his assistant, Walter Cradoc (1610?-59), that the Separatist covenanted congregation at Bristol was founded in 1640, and close links were maintained between the two churches over the next few years. Most significant of all, however, was the claim by a close associate of Wroth and Cradoc, William Erbery (1604-54) of Cardiff, that Llanfaches was formed 'according to the New-England pattern', a pattern which almost invariably involved a church covenant.[58]

Wroth, Cradoc and Erbery were all contemporaries of Vavasor Powell, the most warm-hearted and zealous of the Welsh Puritan preachers. Powell took it for granted that when a new church was formed it would have a covenant as its basis. His description of the normal practice in establishing a church is particularly interesting. First of all, the prospective members should know one another and consider one another to be 'fit materials to make a church'. Due consultations should be undertaken with pastors and members of other churches, and then a day of humiliation set aside during which a register of members' names should be taken. In the course of another day of humiliation the church should be properly constituted in the presence of pastors and members of other congregations. This constituting should include taking and confirming the register of members' names, hearing and approving an account of each member's faith and experience, and then joining together in covenant as follows:

> We do promise and covenant in the presence of the Lord, that the Almighty Jehovah shall be our God; we do give up our selves to serve Him in spirit and in truth, and do promise to walk together as a church, according to the rule of the Gospel, and to watch over one another and continue in fellowship together, and be helpful to each other, as God shall enable us, according to our duties expressed in the word of God.[59]

Unfortunately, it is now virtually impossible to discover whether this description accurately reflects contemporary practice or whether it merely presents Powell's view of the ideal mode of establishing a church. Modern writers have declared that most if not all early Independent churches had covenants, but no general documentary evidence exists for such statements.[60]

What evidence there is suggests that the covenant in Wales was at least as important among the Baptists as among the Independents.[61] The first recorded covenant is that of the Baptist congregation at Llanwenarth-Abergavenny in Gwent. Formed in 1652, the following note is found in the church book:

> The 11th of the 5th month, 1655
>
> The Church this day being met together have renewed their Covenant, viz., that they would walk with one another by the assistance of God, as near as they can according to the Scriptures. And have declared that they do disown all former disorders in any. And also that they do withdraw from all such ministers that do receive maintenance from the magistrates and from all such as consent not to wholesome doctrine, or teach otherwise.[62]

In 1668, a famous and influential Baptist church was established at Rhydwilym on the western borders of Carmarthenshire, the members covenanting with God and with one another. Not until 1700 is there a recorded covenant for a congregation of Independents, the first instance being the covenant of the church at Tirdwncyn or Mynydd-bach in the Llangyfelach district of Swansea.[63]

The nature of the evidence, however, defeats any attempt to trace accurately the extent or development of the practice. Original church books are few and far between. Denominational histories usually speak of churches being formally established without indicating whether a covenant was adopted. Some churches seem to have entered into a modified form of covenant agreement whereby members gave their assent to a confession of faith rather than making specific pledges. In the case of Rhyd-wilym, there was both a confession of faith and a covenant; the former has been preserved, but the latter has disappeared, possibly because it was never in written form. When the church at Cilfowyr, Pembrokeshire, was established in 1704, members agreed to and signed a confession containing fifty-eight articles, three items concerning the discipline to be exercised within the congregation, and the choice of Samuel John to be their elder and pastor. To all intents and purposes agreements of this kind were covenants, although the specific covenant form was absent.[64]

Most of the recorded covenants were made in the eighteenth century, but their dates do not invariably correspond with the actual formation of the church, a fact which again makes an accurate analysis of the practice very difficult. The covenants of the mixed Independent-Baptist church at Llanbryn-mair provide an example of this problem. There had been a church – more 'scattered' than 'gathered' – in that part of Montgomeryshire since the days of Vavasor Powell, but not until 1733 do we find the first definite evidence of a written covenant, probably as the result of the settlement of a new minister at Llanbryn-mair. This new minister, Benjamin Meredith (1700-49), had been a member of the Baptist congregation at Llanwenarth, and there are marked similarities between the Llanbryn-mair covenant of 1733 and the renewed Llanwenarth-Abergavenny covenant of 1655. What cannot now be ascertained, however, is whether there was also a covenant at Llanbryn-mair prior to 1733 – a distinct possibility in the light of Vavasor Powell's influence over its early years – or whether that of 1733 was introduced entirely at the instigation of Benjamin Meredith. It is interesting to add that a new and more detailed covenant was drawn up around the year 1798, when John Roberts (1767-1834) was ordained to take charge of the congregation at Llanbryn-mair.[65]

It appears, therefore, that the personal leanings of a particular church leader, or a consciousness among church members that they were entering a new era, might be responsible for the drawing up of a formal covenant. The influence of the minister was clearly apparent at Wrexham in north-east Wales: the origins of the Baptist church there had probably been laid in the 1650s, but its written covenant dates from 1773 at a time when a greater degree of order was being introduced into the church.[66]

Covenants were still being used in the formation of churches in the nineteenth century. When an English Baptist cause was established at Monmouth in 1818, it is recorded that the members covenanted together 'in the normal way'. John Davies (1803-54) of Mynydd-bach, Llangyfelach, was still emphasizing the importance of the covenant in the 1840s, but its usage seems gradually to have declined.[67] Although many Independent and Baptist churches were formed in the rapidly-growing industrial areas of Glamorgan and Monmouthshire during the first half of the nineteenth century, for example, there is very little specific mention of their having church covenants.[68]

The same decline appears to have affected rural Wales, too. As thorough-going an Independent as Azariah Shadrach (1774-1844), who in a pastoral letter from a gathering of Independent ministers in 1835 could speak of the dangers of breaking the covenant made with God and fellow-believers in joining a church, had some years earlier established a church at Rhydlydan, near Pentrefoelas on the western borders of Clwyd, merely by holding a Bible in his hand and asking prospective members whether or not they intended taking the Word of God as their rule.[69]

Certainly by the early twentieth century the covenant was, with very few exceptions, regarded as a thing of the past. A speaker at the annual meetings of the Union of Welsh Independents in 1916 was at pains to emphasize the abiding significance of the covenant, but the whole tenor of his address shows that the concept had long been neglected among the churches of his denomination.[70] Interestingly enough, around the same time R. B. Jones (1869-1933) was introducing a covenant into the life of the 'semi-independent' Tabernacle Baptist Church at Porth in the Rhondda Valley, in an effort to bind church members together in closer fellowship and more dedicated discipleship. The re-emergence of what was to all intents and purposes a gathered church was in this instance, at least, accompanied by the re-emergence of the church covenant.[71]

* * * * *

It is not so much the history of the church covenant that is of particular interest, however, as its general significance for church life. Most important of all is its bearing on the question of the very nature of the church and in particular the purity of the church. The whole issue of the church covenant was bound up with the principle of the gathered church, the principle that the church should contain only 'visible saints'.[72] This is the reason why the covenant was never adopted by thorough-going Anglicans: their church polity was essentially comprehensive, theoretically embracing every member of society rather than the 'visible saints' of the Separatist groups.

The covenant came to have considerable significance among Presbyterians, especially in Scotland, but because Presbyterianism was also largely comprehensivist in outlook, the covenant was adopted at national level rather than by individual local churches. Thus the well-known National Covenants of 1581 and 1638 bound Scottish Presbyterians to support Reformed doctrine and discipline and to reject all religious changes not approved by a free assembly of the Kirk. The even better-known Solemn League and Covenant of 1643 bound England to establish a Presbyterian system in exchange for Scottish military aid against King Charles I. It was these national covenants which were placed in jeopardy at the restoration of Charles II, and which resulted in the tragic persecution of the 'Covenanters'.[73]

To members of the gathered churches these national covenants were of little significance. They conceived of the church not as a national institution but as a body of believers gathered together in one specific place; and at the heart of this body of believers, defining what was a believer and binding him to his fellow-believers, was the church covenant. This principle is embodied in the opening words of the covenant of the Independent church at Mynydd-bach, Llangyfelach, first drawn up in 1700 and renewed in 1759:

> We do heartily take this one God for our only God and our chief good, and this Jesus Christ for our only Lord, Redeemer and Saviour, and this Holy Ghost for our Sanctifier.

In other words, the church is to comprise those who profess to be within the covenant of grace. Prospective members of Chester Street Baptist Church, Wrexham, were first examined concerning their understanding of the faith and the workings of grace in their hearts; then they were baptized; then they gave their assent to the church covenant. Only afterwards, when their spiritual standing had as far as possible been ascertained, were they admitted to membership and to the Lord's Table.[74]

Some of the early Separatists went so far as to argue that there can be no church without some form of covenant. Henry Jacob, whose ideas indirectly influenced the church at Llanfaches, believed that a church was formed 'by a free mutual consent of believers joining and covenanting to live as members of a holy society together'.

A profession of faith might be all that was necessary to recognize a person as a Christian, but the organization of a church required more than this. In the words of John Robinson (*c*.1575-1625), 'The bare profession of faith makes not a true church, except the persons so professing be united in the covenant and fellowship of the gospel into particular congregations.' Robinson considered that even the preaching of the Word and administration of the sacraments were not of the essence of the church. They might be abused or perverted in churches falsely so called, but the 'Lord's visible covenant' was the *sine qua non* of the true church.[75]

At the same time the purity of the church might be jeopardized by the obvious failure of the boundaries of the covenant of grace and those of the church covenant to correspond perfectly. In the words of Thomas Hooker (1586?-1647), 'A man may be in the covenant of grace, and share in the benefit thereof, who is not in a church state; and a man may be in a church state, who is not really in the covenant of grace.' Circumstances or lack of discernment might prevent a genuine Christian from joining himself to a true body of God's people. On the other hand, a man might be accepted into the covenant fellowship of God's people and yet be a hypocrite and a complete stranger to the grace of God in his heart.

In favour of the covenant, however, it could be argued that a man was less likely to commit himself to specific covenant pledges unless he was assured of his place in the covenant of grace. Similarly, the existence of the covenant provided some form of filter by which the church could separate those deemed to be truly converted from those who had only the name of godliness. Thus William Carey, plagued by recalcitrant members, dissolved his church at Leicester in 1790 and then re-established it on the basis of a covenant 'to bind them to a strict and faithful New Testament discipline, let it affect whom it might'.[76]

This function of the covenant, however, raised fundamental questions about the membership of the church. Was it possible to limit church membership to 'visible saints'? Those who clung to the principle of the gathered church sought to educate prospective members in the faith and in the nature of their covenant obligations. The covenant itself might be a means of such education. The first known congregational covenant in Britain consisted almost entirely of pledges to repudiate the Anglican Church.[77] More usual was the practice of bringing prospective members to a position where they could properly sign the church covenant. There might be certain moral obstacles: at Mynydd-bach, Capel Isaac, near Llandeilo in Carmarthenshire, there was some doubt about Richard Thomas because of a decline in his profession, while Edward John Harry's admission had to be postponed until the church could be assured of his good character. There might also be difficulties in understanding the basic doctrines of the faith:

> Evan Tho. Evan near Cwm y Scafarnog was examined and received to Church Communion at Mynydd Bach the 17th of Feb. 1744-5 [=1745]. He was Examined one month before and we delayed to receive him until we would endeavour to catechize him better and bring him to more knowledge in the fundamentals or principles of religion.

But lack of understanding was not an insurmountable obstacle at this church:

> Gweneiffred David the widow of David Lloyd was received to Church Communion; tho' she was somewhat ignorant yet she had a good character to live inoffensive according to that small measure of knowledge she had received.

Only after being formally screened in this way were candidates for membership allowed to sign the church covenant. And the signing in itself was not only a declaration of intent on the part of the member but also an affirmation of the church's claims over that member.[78]

The role of the covenant in ensuring the purity of the local congregation posed one particular problem for those congregations who believed in baptizing infants. Wales appears to have been spared any significant dilemmas in this respect, but in New England the problem assumed major proportions. It was accentuated by the fact that the colonies were in large measure founded upon the Congregational churches established by the first settlers. There was no inkling of the ensuing crisis during the first generation: churches were formed by 'visible saints' on the basis of covenants, their children were baptized, and it was confidently believed that these children, brought up henceforth in true gospel churches and in godly families, would eventually come to own the covenant for themselves. Sadly, this failed to happen in all cases; but even this failure did not of itself immediately imperil the church structure. The real threat came when the third generation – the children of parents as yet unable to give evidence that they had themselves experienced regeneration – was born. Were these parents truly church members? Should their children also be baptized? If baptism were administered, would it not undermine the accepted practice of baptizing only the seed of believers? On the other hand, if baptism were not administered, a significant proportion of the population would be excluded from the visible church; and this exclusion could have only a detrimental effect on the religious, moral, social and political development of the colony.

Eventually, in 1662, a compromise subsequently known as the 'Half-Way Covenant' was reached. It allowed the baptism of the children of parents who had not made a saving profession of faith, provided that the latter understood the faith, publicly professed their assent to it, refrained from all scandalous living and solemnly owned the baptismal covenant made for them by their parents. Thus was created a partial church membership, whereby certain persons were able to have their children baptized and were subject to church discipline but had no right to partake of the Lord's Supper or to vote in church affairs. This innovatory compromise, welcomed by most churches, provoked no little opposition from more conservative elements in New England and highlighted the tension which could arise in the membership of gathered Paedobaptist congregations over several generations.[79]

Baptist congregations, also constituting gathered churches, had no such problems. Indeed, while many Baptist churches found the use of covenants beneficial, others considered that they were not essential for church membership. What took the place of the covenant, in their view, was the baptism of believers.

This seems to have been an increasing tendency in the thought of John Smyth, a key figure in the growth of Baptist ideas at the beginning of the seventeenth century, although he did not abandon the covenant idea entirely. His former associates and the founders of the first specifically Baptist church in Britain *circa* 1612, Thomas Helwys and John Murton, considered that baptism in effect denied the need for a church covenant: a person entered the visible church by faith and baptism alone. Their church was Arminian in its doctrine; it is likely that the first Particular or Calvinistic Baptist church in Britain, formed in 1633, had a covenant.[80]

Hanserd Knollys (1599?-1691), one of the leaders of the Baptists during the Commonwealth period, challenged the Independents to prove from Scripture the necessity for a church covenant. The only conditions of membership, in his opinion, were faith in Christ, repentance, and willingness to be baptized. Other Baptists echoed his views, although some continued to approve of at least an informal covenant in addition to baptism.[81]

There appears to have been no debate over the issue among Welsh Baptists;[82] indeed, in Wales there are more covenants extant for Baptist churches than for Independent churches. Baptism was, of course, in itself a covenantal act, signifying publicly a determination henceforth to cleave to Christ and to submit to his lordship.

In addition to establishing the purity of the church, the covenant was a means of preserving that purity. Recalcitrant members could be brought to see the error of their ways by reminding them of what they had once pledged to observe. Writing a pastoral letter to Independent churches in 1835, Azariah Shadrach emphasized that neglect of the means of grace was in effect a breaking of the covenant whereby church members pledged themselves to be faithful in carrying on God's cause, to take God's word as their rule and to walk together in the paths of the Lord's commandments.[83]

R. B. Jones was much more specific and explicit in his attempts to preserve the purity of his congregation at Porth. Not only individual members were involved; in a pastoral letter of 1931 he rebuked the whole church for its neglect of the covenant. Non-attendance at meetings, failure to give generously, worldliness, and the loss of a spirit of loving obedience were cited as being among the major examples of breaking covenant pledges. He listed the covenant rules in full and reminded his members of the solemn oath which they had taken before God in agreeing to them. He then went so far as to refuse to administer communion until the church had confessed its sins and promised to honour the covenant.[84]

The covenant might also be employed as a bulwark against false doctrine. In 1750 the Baptist church at Hengoed on the borders of Glamorgan and Monmouthshire sent a letter to the Welsh Baptist Association asking what should be done with those who were covenant-breakers, who had turned to Arminianism, and who had broken those pledges made when received into church membership. The people in question were those who, under the leadership of Charles Winter (1700-73), had left the church for doctrinal reasons and founded another congregation nearby at Craigyfargod. The Association's advice was that they should be formally excommunicated on the grounds of their error, and that no preachers should visit them except with the aim of winning them back to the truth as set out in their original covenant pledges.[85]

One means of seeking to preserve the purity of the church was to arrange a formal renewing of the church covenant. The earliest record of a church covenant in Wales, that of the Llanwenarth-Abergavenny congregation in 1655, was in fact a renewal of a previous covenant in which members declared that 'they do disown all former disorders in any'. The covenant of 1700 at Mynydd-bach, Llangyfelach, was renewed in 1759; that of 1733 at Llanbryn-mair was amplified in 1798.[86]

It is not easy to determine the factors responsible for these renewals and amplifications; ministerial changes seem to have had some influence, but elsewhere the element of disciplining the congregation and awakening members to a new sense of their responsibilities appears to have been particularly prominent. This was certainly the case in Anglesey when Christmas Evans first arrived there. His response to the low condition of the Baptist churches was to call a day of prayer and fasting for the purpose of repentance and the renewing of covenant pledges. At Porth, the Jubilee services of 1924 provided the occasion for R. B. Jones's church to make the following declaration:

> We hereby solemnly and definitely record that we dedicate ourselves afresh to God that He may work His

purpose in and through us both as individuals and collectively.[87]

Perhaps the most striking example of the use of covenant renewal for such purposes is to be found in New England, especially in the wake of the Half-Way Covenant of 1662. The sober realization that all too few of the children of believers were coming to profess publicly faith in Christ, together with other trials, encouraged a wave of covenant renewals by churches, usually with the aim of introducing the Half-Way Covenant, sometimes including a new covenant of reformation and associated with a day of humiliation.[88]

In 1677 Increase Mather (1639-1723) published his *Renewal of Covenant the Great Duty Incumbent on Decaying or Distressed Churches*; and three years later, in *Returning unto God the Great Concernment of a Covenant People*, he claimed that 'the churches which have lately and solemnly attended this Scripture expedient, for reformation, have experienced the presence of God with them, signally owning them therein'. Jonathan Edwards, on the other hand, saw the usefulness of covenant renewal not so much in the reformation of existing evils as in inculcating basic principles of holy living in the new converts brought into the church by the Great Awakening.[89]

* * * * *

If the primary function of the church covenant was the setting forth and the preservation of the purity of the church, it also served the important purpose of encouraging the unity of the church. The bonds of the covenant were designed to promote a sense of belonging and common responsibility one for another. As the members at Llanbryn-mair pledged in 1798:

> We bind ourselves and make a covenant with the Lord, and with one another.[90]

As a result, the covenant could prove an important stimulus to cohesion within the church and to co-operation among the members. This might be of particular significance in scattered rural areas, in the new rootless urban communities, and in recently-settled districts such as New England. For one thing, the covenant threw up a barrier between church members and the world outside. For another, it encouraged an equality between members which bridged all economic, cultural, social and educational differences. There might be a diversity of gifts and of offices in the church, but all members were bound together at the same level by the covenant. In effect, the covenant supplied a practical demonstration that 'there is neither Jew nor Greek, there is neither bond nor free, there is neither male nor female: for ye are all one in Christ Jesus' (Galatians 3:28).

In addition to encouraging an awareness of equality before God, the church covenant also proved a powerful factor in promoting the concept of belonging together within a living fellowship, and in this sense provided a healthy corrective to the ever-present tendencies towards excessive individualism. Nobody saw this more clearly in nineteenth-century Wales than Michael D. Jones (1822-98), one of the most prominent of Welsh Independents. He believed that the Christian life flourished best within a visible, covenantal framework where members were directly responsible to God for their collective conduct. In a spiritual context, this framework was provided by the local church; but covenanted members of one particular congregation were also linked to covenanted members of other assemblies of saints. In his opinion, the same framework was relevant to the political sphere and especially to relationships between nations, and he strove to promote this concept of belonging and interdependence at that level.[91]

Within the local church, this sense of belonging could be very powerful indeed. The public covenant with the church might be deemed stronger than the private covenant with an unbelieving wife, for example, or blood relationships with parents, brothers, sisters, children. The church covenant provided members with spiritual parents, spiritual brothers and sisters, spiritual children. Members were bound to watch over not only their own souls but also the spiritual welfare of their fellow members. Moreover, they were pledged to treat those within the covenant in Christian love and with scrupulous honesty. Here are some of the pledges included in the Llanbryn-mair covenant of 1798 which were intended to promote the unity of the church:

> 7. We promise that we shall not harbour evil thoughts concerning one another without conscientiously ascertaining if we have just cause, and that we shall not believe every tale we hear about one another without sufficient testimony, and especially that we shall not slander one another, but rather that we shall conceal one another's faults in so far as we are able to do so with a good conscience.
>
> 8. We promise according to our gifts and opportunities, to do our utmost to build up one another in the Lord, that is, to pray and keep watch over one another, to be ready to give the best advice and guidance that we can to one another, and to behave kindly and forgivingly to one another according to the law of Christ.
>
> . . . .
>
> 10. We promise carefully to refrain from repeating before unbelievers what is done or spoken in the Church lest we should be guilty of giving that which is holy to dogs and casting pearls before swine.[92]

Only death or excommunication could break the covenant bond. A unilateral decision to leave the covenanted community had in itself no force: the covenant remained in operation even where one member or one party apparently repudiated it, and those remaining faithful to the covenant were duty bound to show the straying sheep the importance of returning to the covenant fold. Where there was serious doctrinal or moral error in direct opposition to covenant pledges, however, excommunication was practised and the covenant held to be inoperative in the case of those excommunicated.[93]

Covenanted unity was sealed by the sacraments. Early Separatists were convinced that the sacraments of the Church of England had no value whatsoever because they were not administered within a believing covenanted community. Indeed, seventeenth-century Independents generally believed that it was the covenant rather than the sacraments which lay at the heart of the church as an institution. One of the most important functions of the sacraments, in their opinion, was the sealing of the covenant. John Robinson, for instance, believed that the covenant should precede baptism both in logic and in chronology, because the sacrament of baptism could be valid only within a covenanted fellowship. Baptists disagreed: in their view, baptism displayed and sealed faith in Christ, and the use of the church covenant was a means only of pledging obedience to Christ in a particular congregation.[94]

But disagreement over the exact interpretation of the meaning and significance of baptism was not necessarily a source of division within the church. Covenant undertakings could, in fact, help to resolve any disunity arising from such disagreement. In 1773 a covenant was drawn up at the Baptist church at Wrexham: henceforth prospective church members were to be baptized on a profession of faith, to sign the covenant, and then to receive Communion. Three years later, however, an additional covenant was instituted for those who were of a Paedobaptist persuasion but were in all other respects in agreement with the doctrines held by the church, admitting them into membership on condition that they pledged not to upset the basic Baptist position held by the church. Where the unity of the church was placed in jeopardy by disagreement over the sacrament intended to consolidate such unity, therefore, the covenant might be an effective means of welding dissenting parties together.[95]

On the whole, the sealing and unifying role of the sacrament of the Lord's Supper received more widespread acceptance. According to one Welsh writer in 1824:

> This [church] covenant has the Lord's supper as a seal upon it. And of every seal ever set upon a covenant, this is the most solemn, the most precious, and the most holy – the flesh and blood of the dear Son of God. When church members meet around the Lord's table, each one sets his hand to the seals, and thus confirms the covenant he made when first he came into God's church.[96]

In both Baptist and Paedobaptist churches the Lord's Supper was regarded as sealing covenant unity. The classic Baptist pattern was to be seen at Wrexham: spiritual examination, baptism, the signing of the covenant, admission to membership and to the Lord's Table. In Paedobaptist congregations the normal expectation was for a person baptized in childhood to subsequently make a profession of faith, to give assent to the church covenant, and then to receive the Lord's Supper.

Only with the gradual decline of spirituality did this sealing function lose its significance. The change may perhaps best be seen in the attitude of Solomon Stoddard (1643-1728/9) of Northampton, New England. Renouncing the entire concept of a church covenant, he declared that he henceforth intended to allow all outwardly godly people to partake of the bread and wine.[97] The re-embracing of the principles underlying the church covenant by Jonathan Edwards, Stoddard's grandson, and his related attempt to ensure that only professed believers should be permitted to take Communion, ultimately resulted in the dismissal of Edwards from Stoddard's former pastorate at Northampton.[98] For Edwards, the Lord's Supper was a sign and a seal of the new covenant, and he would no doubt have agreed with George Lewis, Llanuwchllyn, when he asks: 'How can it be entertained that he should covenant with God who neither understands the new covenant, nor consents to its requirements?' For those who did understand the new covenant and did consent to its requirements, on the other hand, the Lord's Supper served as a means of bringing them together in covenant unity.[99]

* * * * * *

The third main function of the church covenant was the emphasizing of the voluntary nature of the church and the importance of personal commitment to the local congregation. Because they believed that the church extended over the whole nation, neither Anglicans nor Presbyterians had much sympathy with the concept of a church covenant. What the church covenant of the Separatist bodies stressed, however, was that each individual undertook a voluntary commitment to Christ in a particular congregation. In making this commitment, John Penry in effect signed his own death warrant. Even in more enlightened days, the covenant stood as a means of testing and demonstrating the mettle of church members. In the opinion of John Davies of Mynydd-bach, Llangyfelach, for example, entering into church covenant required serious self-examination, hearty resolution, true humility, spiritual desire, self-dedication to God, separation from the world and from all false religion, and a constant determination to follow the Lord. It was not something to be enforced by law or by tradition: attachment to a church was entirely voluntary, to be undertaken with wholehearted personal commitment.[100]

This voluntary element raised important questions concerning the government of the church. A covenant required common consent: was it not the logical conclusion that the consenting members in fact governed the church? Advocates of the covenant argued that Christ was the sole head of each individual congregation; those who engaged in covenant together were pledging themselves to submit to his rule, to walk in his ways, to obey his commandments. The covenant was thus regarded as promoting not so much democracy as theocracy.[101] In practice, however, the covenant certainly encouraged the spread of democratic ideas. In society at large, the covenant principle was one root of the growing interest in government by consent and what later came to be called the 'social contract'. 'All voluntary relations,' declared Richard Mather (1596-1669) in *An Apology for Church Covenant* (1643), 'all relations which are neither natural nor violent, are entered into by way of covenant'; and this tenet formed a basis for Puritan views of the nature of civil government for much of the seventeenth century.[102] Such views could hardly fail to be carried over into the life of the church. The insistence on the voluntary coming together and consenting together imposed a common responsibility on all church members; and responsibility implied a measure of freedom and even authority in determining how best to 'walk with one another . . . according to the Scriptures'.[103]

The problems that might arise from such freedom and authority seem to be indicated by a tendency to make longer and more detailed covenants as time went on. The short, generalized covenants typical of the seventeenth century might be open to all manner of interpretation by members zealous to assert their supposed rights. During the following century, therefore, covenants containing a substantial list of specific pledges became more common, in all probability with the aim of curbing excessive independence.[104] Some covenants even included pledges to accept the authority of a particular leader. One congregation, for example, consented 'to be members of this particular Church of Christ at Tirdwncyn whereof Lewis Davies is pastor and overseer and to submit to his teaching and ministerial guidance and oversight according to God's word'.[105]

One advocate of the church covenant could speak of the relationship between leaders and congregation as 'a speaking *Aristocracy* in the face of a silent *Democracy*',[106] but the body of church members could hardly be wholly or permanently silent. The voluntary element which lay at the heart of the concept of the covenant certainly threw the entire issue of the government of the church into sharp focus. At the same time, the covenant bound both leaders and members together in a common solemn engagement which could not be lightly broken from either side.[107]

Within the congregation, covenant pledges were a direct encouragement to the mutual edification of believers, fruitful church fellowship and holiness of life. By stirring up the 'visible saints' within the framework of the church, the covenant helped to set a high standard for the spiritual life of the church and to stimulate the constituent members to reach and maintain that standard. The covenant might, for example, be a bulwark against backsliding and sin:

> Is he who is a member under this Covenant to God and his people as free in his mind and his conscience to commit sin as if he were not a member? It is not likely; no: when he is tempted, he calls to mind, 'I am a mem-

> ber of Christ's holy church; how shall I commit this great evil and sin against God?' In our church relationship we have those who truly watch over us – those who warn us, who advise us, who rebuke us in love, and who pray for us specifically and earnestly.[108]

More positively, mutual pledges might prove a dynamic incentive to co-operative endeavours in evangelism through the church. As George Lewis realized, the church covenant enabled

> men of various gifts and qualifications to be bound to use together their talents towards bringing about what the body has in mind. 1 Cor. xii. 2. It is possible for many . . . to do more than what one can achieve. Eccles. iv. 10.[109]

When men pledged themselves to strive together on behalf of the faith – 'desire we do and endeavour we will to spread and adorn the interest and ways of the Lord and Saviour Jesus Christ', as the Caerleon covenant puts it[110] – the potential effect on the life and ministry of the church could be immeasurable. In other words, the covenant encouraged a wholehearted engagement with the church. It brought mind, heart and will together in a solemn pledge to serve Christ within Christ's church. The fact that it was a *voluntary* commitment helped to reduce the danger of a nominal attachment to the church. But the fact that it was a *commitment*, and a formal, serious, public commitment at that, brought an element of sober dedication into the churches which is all too conspicuous by its absence in the twentieth century.

* * * * *

There were, of course, a number of objections to the whole concept of the church covenant. The individual church covenant was entirely foreign to the Anglican and Presbyterian ecclesiastical structures; in England, at least, Baptists appear to have been rather ambivalent in their attitude towards it, and there were some Independents who were dubious of its value. Richard Mather, a staunch supporter of the covenant principle, listed the main objections as follows:

> But joining doth not always signify joining in covenant; Philip joined to the eunuch's chariot, and dust to men's feet, Acts 8:29 & Luke 10:11, and yet there was no covenant, and therefore men may join to the church without any covenant . . .
>
> Church covenant is a term that is not found in Scripture . . .
>
> But this church covenant puts some disparagement upon the covenant of grace, which every believer is entered into with God, and seems to charge the same with insufficiency; for every second covenant doth argue that the first was not faultless, Heb. 8:7 . . .
>
> But the Scripture, Acts 2:41, tells of joining to the church without any covenant, for it was not possible that 3000 should enter into covenant in one day . . .
>
> But why is there so little proof of this church covenant in the New Testament?[111]

The unavoidable difficulty was the absence of any specific verse in the New Testament which instructed every church to have a specific covenant, or which proved beyond the shadow of a doubt that one of the early Christian churches had such a covenant. Writers might talk of the church as being a covenant community, members pledging with one another to meet together and uphold the worship of God according to his word, but verses appealed to in support of this position were at best only indirectly relevant and at worst were palpably inadequate to the task.[112] Richard Mather declared confidently that 'the Church Covenant may be proved from the New Testament', yet had to make the following significant qualification: 'But suppose there were not pregnant places for it in the New Testament, yet it is not enough to prove the same unlawful.' He proceeded to argue that those portions of the Old Testament not specifically repealed in the New Testament were of abiding force, and that the covenant fell into this category. The line of reasoning pursued by John Cotton (1584-1652) was a little different: because the New Testament was written at a time when civil authorities were often opposed to the gospel, references to the covenant were always made obliquely, by using 'parables and similitudes', so that these authorities would not suspect any unlawful leaguing together which might ostensibly imperil the peace.[113]

These were hardly powerful arguments, and without unequivocal scriptural support the supporters of the church covenant were clearly at a disadvantage. And yet the whole idea of a gathered church, a church of 'visible saints', presupposes some form of covenant engagement: a joining together with other believers before God, a voluntary commitment to the aims of the church, a personal consenting to abide by the order and discipline of the congregation. Even a convinced Presbyterian like Lewis Edwards could admit that a true church exists where 'personal subjects of Christ, or at least those professing as much, voluntarily bind themselves as fellow-subjects the one to the other'.[114] James Bannerman (1807-68), a forthright opponent of Independency, nevertheless acknowledged that an implicit covenant lay at the heart of the visible church:

> By whatever name it may be called, this outward relationship with Christ is, to all intents and purposes, a covenant or federal one. We have the two distinguish-

> ing characteristics of a covenant, – namely, first, certain outward conditions enjoined; and, second, certain outward promises annexed to a compliance with these conditions. On the one side, we have an outward profession of faith and an entrance within a Church state, as the conditions fulfilled on the part of those who join themselves to the Christian society; and on the other side, we have, as following upon this fulfilment, the bestowment of certain outward privileges, to be enjoyed by the members of the Church in its ministry, ordinances, and administration.[115]

The implicit covenant basis of the church being allowed, it was the need for an explicit covenant for each individual congregation that was rejected. In particular, it was the attempt to make an explicit covenant obligatory that aroused the opposition of other church groupings. Presbyterians might admit that the church covenant was 'a prudential humane device to keep the members together, which in some places and cases may haply be of good use'; what they would not concede was that there could be no true church where there was no such covenant.[116]

As in the case of the personal covenant, therefore, the explicit church covenant might be found useful and beneficial but should never be held to be binding on all congregations. The true church might indeed be founded on an implicit covenant; an explicit covenant might serve the interests of the church very well; but to argue that every church was strictly bound to adopt a formal covenant was to step beyond the bounds of Scripture.

Perhaps the whole question of the necessity for and the value of the covenant can be summed up in the words of the 'Cambridge Platform' adopted by the early Congregational churches of New England. Referring to the church covenant which was so prominent a feature of ecclesiastical life there, it declares:

> Although the more express and plain it is, the more fully it puts us in mind of our mutual duty, and stirreth us up to it, and leaveth less room for the questioning of the truth of the church-estate of a company of professors, and the truth of membership of particular persons: yet we conceive, the substance of it is kept where there is a real agreement and consent of a company of faithful persons to meet constantly together in one congregation for the public worship of God and their mutual edification: which real agreement and consent they do express by their constant practice in coming together for their public worship of God, and by their religious subjection unto the ordinances of God there: the rather, if we do consider how Scripture covenants have been entered into, not only expressed by word of mouth, but by sacrifice; by handwriting and seal; and also sometimes by silent consent, without any writing, or expression of words at all.[117]

Let every church be fully persuaded in its own mind. But a prayerful consideration of the issues involved might prove a valuable means of clearing away the accretions of unbiblical tradition and indifferent habit, thereby promoting that 'real agreement and consent of a company of faithful persons to meet constantly together in one congregation for the public worship of God and their mutual edification' which lies at the very heart of the church.

CONCLUSION

The issues raised by the practice of covenanting, and particularly by the church covenant, are of general historical interest. The quest for a pure church, cleansed from human traditions, unscriptural doctrines and unregenerate members, was one of the most important factors influencing the religious history – and indeed the political history – of the sixteenth and seventeenth centuries in Britain and America, for example. The social bond given visible expression in a community held together by an explicit covenant was also of no little importance in the midst of the political, economic and religious upheavals of that period. At the same time, while emphasizing organic, cohesive virtues, the covenant demonstrated too the importance of individual responsibility. Emerging in an age when the human will was being allowed more and more freedom to express itself, it was not altogether accidental that the covenant was linked to theories of constitutional limitation and government by consent. These and related issues have often been the subject of analysis by American historians; perhaps they deserve more attention on this side of the Atlantic.

Covenanting is also of importance to the individual Christian, however. After all, neither personal covenants nor church covenants were drawn up primarily for the sake of posterity, for study by historians of subsequent centuries. Their essential purpose was instead spiritual: they were solemn engagements with God himself, and as such they should be treated with due respect. In the development of spirituality they occupy a most important place, reflecting as they do the more serious, careful, responsible elements in the Christian faith, while infusing them with a decided urgency, earnestness and commitment. It is these very elements which in the present century, at least, have been increasingly at a premium. At the same time, there has been a corresponding surge in the desire for superficial spiritual thrills, for the glossy and gimmicky in religion. It may be that a renewed interest in covenant theology, and a renewed awareness of the value of covenanting with God, will help to bring his people back to their spiritual roots.

Renewed interest in covenant theology and renewed awareness of the value of covenanting do not, of course, always go together. Recent indications of the former are, in this writer's opinion, greatly to be welcomed. The republication of spiritual classics from our Christian heritage, almost all of them written within a doctrinal framework which had the covenant as one of its principal pillars, should be cause for heartfelt gratitude to God. There is always a danger, however, that a return to doctrinal Christianity – to a robust, virile, forthright and uncompromising stand for biblical truth and to a renewed delight in God's comprehensive plan of salvation – is made without an accompanying return to sound Christian experience and wholehearted Christian living. It is in these two last-named spheres that the covenant has particular relevance to the contemporary situation, challenging believers at the end of the twentieth century to a more earnest and a more thorough commitment to the full-orbed Christian faith. If the recovery of spirituality in the church is one of the foremost needs of our age, the covenant may yet have an important role to play in bringing Christians to a deeper consciousness of the essence of true spirituality, namely a solemn engagement with God himself.

Having said that, it is worth reiterating that Scripture nowhere commands Christians to make a covenant with God. Because covenants are not commanded in Scripture, they are not obligatory for either individuals or churches, and any attempt to make them obligatory would promote only an unbiblical legalism. This danger, however, should not blind us to the fact that an implicit covenant lies at the very heart of a Christian's relationship with God at both individual and church levels. At the personal level, when he takes God to be his God, when he takes Christ to be his Saviour and his Lord, he is entering into a covenant engagement. In joining a congregation he is in effect agreeing to do what those Christians at Llanwenarth-Abergavenny covenanted to do in 1655, namely to 'walk with one another by the assistance of God, as near as they can according to the Scriptures'. *Every* Christian has entered into covenant with God, whether he is aware of the fact or not. It would be no little encouragement to the cause of true spiritual religion were every Christian indeed to appreciate the nature and implications of that covenant undertaking more fully, and to honour his covenant engagement more wholeheartedly.

There may be no scriptural command to make a formal, specific, written covenant, but it cannot be denied that Scripture contains examples of God's people covenanting thus – and doing so voluntarily, freely, willingly, readily. The question may well be asked: if Old Testament saints could respond in this manner to the grace of God as manifested in the old covenant, should those who have a gracious interest in 'the mediator of a better covenant, which was established upon better promises' (Hebrews 8:6) be found wanting in their response? The earnestness, the eagerness, the wholeheartedness, the commitment of these Old Testament believers, and of the saints down the centuries, stand as a challenge to God's people today. And hand-in-hand with that challenge comes encouragement:

> So they gathered themselves together at Jerusalem in the third month, in the fifteenth year of the reign of Asa

> . . . And they entered into a covenant to seek the LORD God of their fathers with all their heart and with all their soul . . . And they sware unto the LORD with a loud voice, and with shouting, and with trumpets, and with cornets. And all Judah rejoiced at the oath: for they had sworn with all their heart, and sought him with their whole desire; and he was found of them: and the LORD gave them rest round about (2 Chronicles 15: 10,12,14-15).

And that same blend of challenge and encouragement is to be found in Charles Wesley's vibrant covenant hymn, based on Jeremiah 50:5:

Come, let us use the grace divine,
  And all, with one accord,
In a perpetual covenant join
  Ourselves to Christ the Lord:

Give up ourselves, through Jesu's power,
  His name to glorify;
And promise, in this sacred hour,
  For God to live and die.

The covenant we this moment make
  Be ever kept in mind:
We will no more our God forsake,
  Or cast his words behind.

We never will throw off his fear
  Who hears our solemn vow;
And if thou art well-pleased to hear,
  Come down, and meet us now.

Thee, Father, Son, and Holy Ghost,
  Let all our hearts receive!
Present with the celestial host,
  The peaceful answer give!

To each the covenant blood apply,
  Which takes our sins away;
And register our names on high,
  And keep us to that day.

APPENDIX A

Examples of Personal Covenants

January 1 1702. – The covenant of grace being a new covenant, because *ever* new, and often to be renewed, I have, this new year's day, early in the morning, while it is yet dark, solemnly renewed it upon my knees, and be it a memorandum indeed, ever remembered, and never forgotten.

Humbly acknowledging my dependence upon God, as my Creator and the Author of my being; my obligations in duty to him as my Sovereign Lord and Ruler, and my engagements in gratitude to him as my Protector and Benefactor; and mentioning, with thankfulness, the many mercies of my life hitherto, and particularly those of the year past; during which, I have found myself the care of a very kind Providence, which has made the steps of my pilgrimage comfortable; which has preserved to me the use of my reason and understanding, limbs and senses; hath continued my liberty and opportunity to exercise my ministry; hath provided plentifully for me and my family, and loaded me daily with his benefits. For all which I praise his name, and for the mediation of Jesus Christ, to which I owe all.

Acknowledging also, and lamenting the remaining strength of my corruptions, and my bent to backslide from the living God, taking to myself the shame of my many defects and follies, notwithstanding my frequent renewing of my covenant with God, and flying to Christ for righteousness, pardon, and peace.

I once more bind my soul with a bond to be the Lord's wholly, and only, and for ever his. Into thy hands, O God, I commit my spirit, to be ruled, cleansed, and sanctified throughout, qualified for thy service in this world, and for the fruition of thee in the other. My body I present unto thee a living sacrifice, holy and acceptable, for it is my reasonable service. My ministry I devote to thine honour, and the continuance and success of it I submit to thy will. All my worldly comforts I lay at thy feet to be disposed of as thou pleasest. My life itself is thine. O God of my life, 'my times are in thy hand.' Whatever may be the events of this year, let divine grace be sufficient for me, to enable me to accommodate myself to the will of God in them; and then nothing can come amiss. If God will be with me and keep me in the way that I go, throughout the remaining part of my pilgrimage, in the world where I am but a stranger, and will give me bread to eat and raiment to put on, and a heart to love him, and serve him, and live to him, so that I may come at last to my heavenly Father's house in peace, then shall the Lord be my God, my Lord, and my God for ever. Amen. Hallelujah.

MATTHEW HENRY.

Source: J. B. Williams, *The Lives of Philip and Matthew Henry* (1678 and 1828; republished, Edinburgh: Banner of Truth Trust, 1974), 'Matthew Henry', 80-1.

* * * * *

MATTHEW HENRY (2)

1703, January 1. – 'Looking for the blessed hope.' This new-year's day I have in much weakness, and compassed about with many infirmities, upon my knees, made a fresh surrender of myself, my whole self, all I am, all I have, all I can do, to God the Father, Son, and Holy Ghost, my Creator, owner, ruler, and benefactor; all my affections to be ruled by the divine grace, and all my affairs to be overruled by the divine providence, so that I may not come short of glorifying God in this world, and being glorified with him in a better.

Confirming and ratifying all former resignations of myself to God, and lamenting all the disagreeableness of my heart and life therewith, and depending upon the merit of the Redeemer to make this and all my other services acceptable, and the grace of the Sanctifier to enable me to make good these engagements, I again bind my soul with a bond to the Lord, and commit myself entirely to him; particularly, as to the events of this year which I am now entering upon, not knowing the things that may abide me in it.

If this year should be a year of continued health and comfort, I commit myself to the grace of God to be preserved from carnal security, and to be enabled in a day of prosperity to serve God with joy.

If my opportunities, as a minister, should be this year continued, I commit my studies, and ministerial labours at home and abroad, to the blessing of God; having afresh consecrated them all to his service and honour, earnestly desiring mercy of the Lord to be faithful and successful.

If I should be this year at any time tried with doubts concerning my duty, I commit myself to the divine conduct, with an unbiassed desire, praying to know what God will have me to do, with a fixed resolution by his grace to follow his direction in the integrity of my heart.

If I should this year be afflicted in my body, family, name, or estate, I commit my all to the Divine disposal. The will of the Lord be done; only begging that the grace of God may go along with the providence of God in all my afflictions, to enable me both to bear them well, and to use them well.

If this year I should be disturbed, or molested in the exercise of my ministry, if I should be silenced, or otherwise suffer for well doing, I commit the keeping of my soul to God as a faithful Creator; depending upon him to guide me in my call to suffer, and to make that clear, and to preserve me from perplexing snares; depending upon him to support and comfort me under my sufferings, and to bring glory to himself out of them; and then, welcome his whole will.

If this year should be my dying year, as perhaps it may be, I commit my spirit into the hands of my Redeemer, to be washed with his blood, and presented in his arms with exceeding joy. My wife and children I commit to him to be owned, blessed, and preserved by him when I am gone. 'In thee, O Lord, have I put my trust, let me never be ashamed.'

Source: J. B. Williams, *The Lives of Philip and Matthew Henry* (1678 and 1828; republished, Edinburgh: Banner of Truth Trust, 1974), 'Matthew Henry', 83-4.

* * * * *

MICHAEL ROBERTS

Having suffered injury many a time because of my misbehaviour towards God and men in my life as a professor [of religion], I acknowledge my sin and repent of it; and I acknowledge my sinfulness and my guilt, disabling me from thinking or doing that which is good, except as the Spirit of God directs me to that end. I today, in the presence of God, vow to live as follows, and earnestly plead with God to fill me with his grace and to lead me by his Holy Spirit:

1\.

I resolve, by the grace of God, to maintain fellowship with God, as a repentant sinner in the face of the great Atonement, and to live upon the fulness which is in Christ, and to betake myself to his blessed Sacrifice to answer my guilt, and to Christ as Prophet to answer my darkness, and as King to answer my corruptions.

2\.

I resolve, by the grace of God, to make conscientious use of the ordinances of the Gospel, personally between God and myself, and within my family as far as I am able, wherever I may be, and publicly at whatever place and time I may be called upon to do so; and particularly to keep up secret prayers.

3.

I resolve, by the grace of God, that I will search the Bible as my life's chief study, and that I will read some portion of it every day, and take every advantage of the works of authors within my reach with the aim of increasing my knowledge in God's Word.

4.

I resolve, by the grace of God, to sanctify the Sabbath, in thought, word and deed.

5.

I resolve that my behaviour and my communion with my brethren and my nonprofessing fellow-sinners shall be such as is consistent with the Gospel, and without affliction to myself, and edifying and profitable to them.

6.

I resolve, by the grace of God, that I shall not rush into anything, or change my situation in life, or remove my livelihood, or anything of that sort, without enquiring much of the Bible, and seeking advice from my parents and brethren.

7.

I resolve, by the grace of God, that I shall not be a slanderer, or a flatterer, or doubletongued, or tell any untruth; but that I shall endeavour to be pure from the blood of all men in the great Judgement.

8.

I resolve, by the grace of God, while I minister in the

Church, to concentrate on the true doctrine and discipline; and that I shall not be jealous at the elevation of any of my brethren, but rather shall labour to fill my position for God, rightly using my talents in the light of the day of account.

9.

I resolve, by the grace of God, to observe carefully God's Providence, in respect of the Kingdom, the Church, and Families, and especially in respect of myself.

10.

I resolve, by the grace of God, that I shall not misuse any of my precious time, but rather shall spend it in the manner in which I should have desired to spend it when giving my detailed account [to God].

11.

I resolve, by the grace of God, to be faithful and honest in my calling, and to keep a conscience void of offence toward God and men.

12.

I resolve, by the grace of God, that I shall not be miserly, or wasteful, concerning the mercies of this life, but shall eat and dress as is seemly; and shall contribute to the cause of the Gospel, and be charitable, as God has prospered me.

13.

I resolve, by the grace of God, never to eat or drink or sleep to excess, not to do any injury to my nature in any way, as far as I am aware.

14.

I resolve, by the grace of God, to do those things concerning which there is no specific commandment in the Bible in accordance with the general commandments:

'Let all things be done in love.'
'Let all things be done in order.'
'Let all things be done unto edifying.'

Penmount MICHAEL ROBERTS.
October 11th, 1803

I vow to read and to consider these often and bind myself by oath to stand by them conscientiously. And how precious to me is that word, 'My grace is sufficient for thee.'

Source: John Jones, *Cofiant . . . y Parch. Michael Roberts, Pwllheli* (Pwllheli: Robert Owen, 1883), 15-17. It was also published in *Cymru*, IV, 279.

* * * * *

CHRISTMAS EVANS (1)

I. I give my soul and body unto Thee, Jesus, the true God, and everlasting life; deliver me from sin, and from eternal death, and bring me into life everlasting. Amen. – C.E.

II. I call the day, the sun, the earth, the trees, the stones, the bed, the table, and the books, to witness that I come unto Thee, Redeemer of sinners, that I may obtain rest for my soul from the thunders of guilt and the dread of eternity. Amen. – C.E.

III. I do, through confidence in Thy power, earnestly entreat Thee to take the work into Thine own hand, and give me a circumcised heart, that I may love Thee; and create in me a right spirit, that I may seek thy glory. Grant me that principle which Thou wilt own in the day of judgment, that I may not then assume pale-facedness, and find myself a hypocrite. Grant me this, for the sake of Thy most precious blood. Amen. – C.E.

IV. I entreat Thee, Jesus, the Son of God, in power grant me, for the sake of Thy agonizing death, a covenant interest in Thy blood, which cleanseth; in Thy righteousness, which justifieth; and in Thy redemption, which delivereth. I entreat an interest in Thy blood, for Thy *blood's* sake, and a part in Thee, for Thy Name's sake, which Thou hast given among men. Amen. – C.E.

V. O Jesus Christ, Son of the living God, take, for the sake of Thy cruel death, my time, and strength, and the gifts and talents I possess; which, with a full purpose of heart, I consecrate to Thy glory in the building up of Thy Church in the world, for Thou art worthy of the hearts and talents of all men. Amen. – C.E.

VI. I desire Thee, my great High Priest, to confirm, by Thy power from Thy High Court, my usefulness as a preacher, and my piety as a Christian, as two gardens nigh to each other; that sin may not have place in my heart to becloud my confidence in Thy righteousness, and that I may not be left to any foolish act that may occasion my gifts to wither, and I be rendered useless before my life ends. Keep Thy gracious eye upon me, and watch over me, O my Lord, and my God for ever! Amen. – C.E.

VII. I give myself in a particular manner to Thee, O Jesus Christ the Saviour, to be preserved from the falls into which many stumble, that Thy name (in Thy cause) may not be blasphemed or wounded, that my peace may not be injured, that Thy people may not be grieved, and that Thine enemies may not be hardened. Amen. – C.E.

VIII. I come unto Thee, beseeching Thee to be in covenant with me in my ministry. As Thou didst prosper

Bunyan, Vavasor Powell, Howell Harris, Rowlands, and Whit[e]field, O do Thou prosper me. Whatsoever things are opposed to my prosperity, remove them out of the way. Work in me everything approved of God for the attainment of this. Give me a heart 'sick of love' to Thyself, and to the souls of men. Grant that I may experience the power of Thy Word before I deliver it, as Moses felt the power of his own rod, before he saw it on the land and waters of Egypt. Grant this, for the sake of Thine infinitely precious blood, O Jesus, my hope, and my all in all. Amen. – C.E.

IX. Search me now, and lead me into plain paths of judgment. Let me discover in this life what I am before Thee, that I may not find myself of another character when I am shown in the light of the immortal world, and open my eyes in all the brightness of eternity. Wash me in Thy redeeming blood. Amen. – C.E.

X. Grant me strength to depend upon Thee for food and raiment, and to make known my requests. O let Thy care be over me as a covenant-privilege betwixt Thee and myself, and not like a general care to feed the ravens that perish, and clothe the lily that is cast into the oven; but let Thy care be over me as one of Thy family, as one of Thine unworthy brethren. Amen. – C.E.

XI. Grant, O Jesus, and take upon Thyself the preparing of me for death, for Thou art God; there is no need but for Thee to speak the word. If possible, Thy will be done; leave me not long in affliction, nor to die suddenly, without bidding adieu to my brethren, and let me die in their sight, after a short illness. Let all things be ordered against the day of removing from one world to another, that there be no confusion nor disorder, but a quiet discharge in peace. O grant me this, for the sake of Thine agony in the garden. Amen. – C.E.

XII. Grant, O blessed Lord, that nothing may grow and be matured in me to occasion Thee to cast me off from the service of the sanctuary, like the sons of Eli; and for the sake of Thine unbounded merit, let not my days be longer than my usefulness. O let me not be like lumber in a house in the end of my days, in the way of others to work. Amen. – C.E.

XIII. I beseech Thee, O Redeemer, to present these my supplications before the Father; and oh, inscribe them in Thy Book with Thine own immortal pen, while I am writing them with my mortal hand in my book on earth. According to the depths of Thy merit, Thine undiminished grace, and Thy compassion, and Thy manner unto Thy people, O attach Thy Name in Thine Upper Court to these unworthy petitions; and set Thine Amen to them, as I do on my part of the covenant. Amen. – CHRISTMAS EVANS, Llangevni, Anglesea. April 10, 18 - -.

Source: Paxton Hood, *Christmas Evans: The Preacher of Wild Wales* (London: Hodder and Stoughton, 1883), 78-80. Petition XI was granted to the letter – see *ibid.*, 300-3.

* * * * *

CHRISTMAS EVANS (2)

While returning from a place called Tongwynlas, over Caerphilly Mountain, the spirit of prayer descended, very copiously, upon me. I wept for some hours, and heartily supplicated Jesus Christ, for the blessings here following. I found, at this time, a particular nearness to Christ, as if He was close by me, and my mind was filled with strong confidence that He attended to my requests, for the sake of the merits of His own name. This decided me in favour of Cardiff.

I. Grant me the great favour of being led by Thee, according to Thy will – by the directions of Thy providence, and Word, and this disposing of my own mind, by Thy Spirit, for the sake of Thine infinitely precious blood. Amen. – C.E.

II. Grant, if I am to leave Caerphilly, that the gale (of the Spirit's influence), and religious revival I had there, may follow me to Cardiff, for the sake of Thy great name. Amen. – C.E.

III. Grant Thy blessing upon bitter things, to brighten, and quicken me, more and more, and not to depress, and make me more lifeless. Amen. – C.E.

IV. Suffer me not to be trodden under the proud feet of members, or deacons, for the sake of Thy goodness. Amen. – C.E.

V. Grant me the invaluable favour of being, in Thy hand, the means of calling sinners unto Thyself, and of edifying Thy saints, wherever Thou wilt send me, for the sake of Thy name. Amen. – C.E.

VI. If I am to stay at Caerphilly, give me some tokens, as to Gideon of old, by removing the things that discourage me, and are in the way of the prosperity of religion, in that church. Amen. – C.E.

VII. Grant, Lord of glory, and Head of Thy Church, that the Ark of the cause which is Thine, in Anglesea, and Caerphilly, may be sustained from falling into the hands of the Philistines. Do not reject it. Aid it speedily, and lift up the light of Thy countenance upon it; and by Thy Spirit, Word, and providence, so operate, as to carry things forward in the churches, and neighbourhoods, in such a manner as will produce changes in officers, and measures, that will accomplish a thorough improvement, in the great cause, for the establishment of which, in the world, Thou hast died, – and by scattering those that delight in war, and closing the mouths of those that occasion confusion. Amen. – C.E.

VIII. Grant me way-tokens, by the time I begin my journey to Liverpool, and from thence to Anglesea, if it is Thy will that I should go thither this year. Amen. – C.E.

IX. Oh, grant me succour, beneath the shadow of the sympathy that is in Thee, toward them who are tempted, and the unbounded power there is in Thee, to be the relief of such. Amen. – C.E.

X. Accept of my thanksgiving, a hundred millions of times, that Thou hast not hitherto cast me from Thine hand, as a darkened star, or a vessel in which there is no pleasure; and suffer not my life to be extended beyond my usefulness. Thanks that Thou hast not given me a prey to the teeth of any. Blessed be Thy name. Amen. – C.E.

XI. For the sake of Thine infinite merit, do not cast me, Thy servant, under the feet of pride, and injustice, or *worldly* greatness, riches, and selfish oppression of any men, but hide me in the secret of Thy tabernacle, from the strife of tongues. Amen. – C.E.

XII. Help me to wait silently, and patiently upon Thee, for the fulfilment of these things, and not become enraged, angry, and speak unadvisedly with my lips, like Moses, the servant of the Lord. Sustain my heart from sinking, to wait for fresh strength from Zion. Amen. – C.E.

XIII. Help me to wait upon Thee, for the necessaries of life; let Thy mercy, and goodness follow me, while I live; and, as it hath pleased Thee to honour me greatly, by the blessing Thou hast vouchsafed upon the ministry through me, as an humble instrument, at Caerphilly, after the great storm had beaten upon me in Anglesea, like Job, grant that this honour may continue to follow me the remainder of my days, as Thou didst unto Thy servant Job. Amen. – C.E.

XIV. Let this covenant abide, like the covenant of salt, until I come to Thee, in the world of eternal light. I entreat aid to resign myself to Thee, and to Thy will. I beseech Thee, take my heart, and inscribe upon it a deep reverence of Thyself, with an inscription, that time, and eternity cannot efface. Oh, let the remainder of my sermons be taken, by Thee, from my lips; and those which I write, let them be unto Thee for a praise. Unto Thee I dedicate them. If there should be anything, in them, conducive to Thy glory, and to the service of Thy kingdom, do Thou preserve it, and reveal it unto men; else, let it die, like the drops of a bucket in the midst of the scorching heat of Africa. Oh, grant that there may be a drop of that water, which Thou alone canst impart, and which springs up to eternal life running through all my sermons. In this covenant, which, probably, is the last that will be written between me and Thee, on the earth, I commit myself, my wife, and the churches amongst whom I have preached, to the protection of Thy grace, and the care of Thy covenant. Amen. – C.E.

XV. Let this covenant continue, when I am in sickness, or in health, or in any other circumstance; for Thou hast overcome the world, fulfilled the law, finished justifying righteousness, and hast swallowed up death in victory, and all power, in heaven and earth, is in Thy hand. For the sake of Thy most precious blood, and perfect righteousness, note this covenant, with Thine own blood, in the court of the memorials of forgiving mercy: attach unto it

Thy name, in which I believe; and here I, this day, set my unworthy name unto it, with my mortal hand. Amen. – CHRISTMAS EVANS. Dated Cardiff, April 24th, 1829.

Source: Paxton Hood, *Christmas Evans: The Preacher of Wild Wales* (London: Hodder and Stoughton, 1883), 277-80.

* * * * *

THOMAS RICHARD

Upon the consideration that it is in life and health – before the advent of death, the king of terrors, and that great battle in which there is no discharge, when all my senses might be confused and my whole nature disabled by the grievous pains of death – that I should endeavour to settle things surely and firmly between myself and the Lord, making my judgement and my cause aright, I today, the 26th of June, in the year 1834, and the 51st year of my life, make a covenant with my Lord, and with my own hand write out this covenant with my God, and confess with my lips saying:

O Lord God of heaven and earth, which hath made the sea, and the dry land, and the springs of water; the Lord God of Abraham, Isaac, and Jacob, who didst deliver thy people out of the land of Egypt by the hand of Moses and Aaron, and also out of the land of Babylon by the hand of Nebuchadnezzar and Darius at the set time; who didst also, of thine infinite mercy and grace, in the fulness of time send thine only Son Jesus Christ into the world, made of a woman and under the law, to redeem them that were under the law, that we might receive the adoption; in thy sight, in thy presence, and before thee, as was the custom of thy people in all ages when they covenanted with their God.

I first of all confess the guilty state of my person, the just object of eternal damnation, and the thorough corruption of my nature, so that there is nothing pure or whole from head to toe; I am an original and an actual breaker of thy righteous and holy law in body and soul every minute of my life.

Secondly, I have no hope of salvation from anything that I am, or have, or can do myself, and therefore I earnestly desire the divine power of the Holy Ghost to work within me as in all those who believe, that I might without wavering trust only in thy salvation, which is in Christ Jesus – his obedience for my righteousness, his blood for my cleansing, his Spirit to dwell in me and guide me, his name to be a tower unto me for my safety, and to keep me from falling, and to set me before him without blemish; in this I humbly desire in the dust (my proper position) to be without hypocrisy. Do I not hear a cry from heaven, from the lips of the Lord, in reply? 'And I shall make an everlasting covenant with thee, even the sure mercies of David. I will accept him. I will rejoice in him. I will receive him. I will be his father, and he shall be my son, saith the Lord Almighty; and him that cometh to me I will in no wise cast out.' O wonder, from the lips of God to such a miserable creature!

Thirdly, I wholly give up myself, body and soul, time and possessions, unto thee, O my God, and unto thy service alone. Allow me to be in thy hand that I may be secure and useful; and to be at thy feet that I may be in my proper position, the object of thy good pleasure and receive of thy beauty, and to accept thy words for all my wisdom and direction, for all my comfort and enjoyment. If I have run without being sent, forgive, forgive, I pray; but because workers are needed for the harvest, here I am, send me clearly, mightily, and unmistakably. O my Lord, may I, yea, I the most miserable of all, hear from thy holy lips, 'Behold, I have put my spirit upon him; behold, I will be with thy mouth, and shall make my words in thy mouth fire.' May this be a covenant between us for the great work of my ministry? Let not my Lord be angry if I plead thy power and thy faithfulness and these thy promises in support of me in this weighty task. I lean upon thy word for thy satisfaction in this.

Fourthly, I commit my dear wife for ever to thy care, thou who didst declare that thou art Judge of the widows in thy holy habitation. O let not my Lord be angry with me for asking thee to judge her judgement, to judge concerning her, to judge on her behalf, and to judge unto her. I humbly take the word thou didst speak, 'Whatever ye shall ask the Father in my name, he will give it you', as thine answer to me in this covenant.

Fifthly, O Lord, is it not thy word that says, 'Lo, children are an heritage of the Lord: and the fruit of the womb is his reward'? Therefore, in accordance with thy word, I humbly desire to commit the two children that you have given me, Dafydd and Bridget by name, to be thy special possession, children unto God through the effective and gracious calling of the gospel, and to be pillars in God's temple for ever.

O let not my Lord be angry with me for asking that the boy Dafydd shall be like the boy Samuel, serving before the Lord all the days of his life; and like David, the sweet singer of Israel, a man after God's own heart; and to be faithful to God like Shadrach, Mesach, and Abednego; and to be beloved by God like Daniel, a man greatly beloved; and to be a follower of God like a beloved child; and to be a beloved disciple of Christ as was John, who leaned on his Lord's bosom. In the light of this, are there not the makings of a covenant from thee, my Lord, in thy holy word, where thou dost say, 'I shall be a God unto thee, and to thy seed after thee; sanctify unto me all the firstborn; the firstborn of thy sons shall thou give unto me; all the firstborn are mine.' O my Lord, take him; behold, I engage in a new covenant with thee for him, in a renewal of the former one, which I made with thee on the day of his birth; behold, I put my trust in thee, I wait entirely upon thee, and rest upon thee wholly for thy free mercy towards him through Jesus Christ the Mediator.

O let not my Lord be angry with me for asking that my only daughter Bridget, for the sake of the Lord Jesus, should be like Miriam, leading the worship of God; and like Sarah as a mother in Israel; like Deborah to sing of the salvation of the Lord; like Hannah in the house of the Lord; and like Bathsheba, from whom descended the Lord; like Mary, the mother of the Lord, laying up his words in her heart; and like that Mary at the Lord's feet, washing them with her tears and drying them with the hair of her head. O Lord, are there not the makings of a covenant for this girl between me and thee in the words which thou didst speak, 'Suffer little children to come unto me; for of such is the kingdom of heaven.'

O let not my Lord be angry with me – I am but dust and ashes – for thus entering into covenant with thee now. I leave myself, my wife, and my two children, in time, in death, and for eternity, in thy hand. In the same manner I desire that thou wilt be a forgiving God, in Christ, unto me and unto them for ever and ever. Amen and Amen.

Source: Edward Matthews, *Bywgraffiad y Parch. Thos. Richard, Abergwaen* (Abertawe, 1863), 179-80.

APPENDIX B

Examples of Church Covenants

MYNYDD-BACH, LLANGYFELACH (SWANSEA), 1700

(renewed 1759)

We do heartily take this one God for our only God and our chief good and this Jesus Christ for our only Lord Redeemer and Saviour and this holy Ghost for our Sanctifier and the doctrine by him revealed and sealed by his miracles and now contained in the holy Scriptures We do take for the law of God and the Rule of our faith and life and repenting unfeignedly of our Sins we do resolve through the Grace of God Sincerely to obey him both in holiness to God and righteousness to men and in speciall love to the Saints and Comunion with them against all the temptations of the Devil the world and our own flesh and this to the death.

We do consent to be members of this particular Church of Christ at Tirdunkin where of Lewis Davies is pastor and overseer and to submitt to his teaching and ministerial Guidance and oversight according to God's word and to hold Communion with this Church in the publick worshipping of God and to submitt to the brotherly admonition of fellow-members that so we may be built up in knowledge and Holiness and may the better maintain our obedience to Christ and the welfare of this Society and hereby may the more please and Glorify God.

Source: National Library of Wales Ms. 369A.

* * * * *

CAERLEON (GWENT), 1771

We whose Names are below having had our Dismissions from the Churches meeting at Bethesda in Basaleg and Penygarn near Pontypool &c. in order to be constituted an independent Church at Caerleon under the same Denomination (Baptists) & holding the same Principles as we did before in the Churches we belonged to.

In the Name and fear of the Lord; and according to the golden Rule of his Word and the Dictates of our own Consciences, we will Endeavour, and it is our firm Resolusion to fulfill & live under the Influence of the following Articles. Viz;

1. We believe that there is a God: and that he has Authority over all his Creatures: therefore it is the Duty of his reasonable Creatures to obey him in the whole of his revealed Will.

2. Therefore in a solemn and very Religious manner we give ourselves unto the Lord, Bodies & Souls, to be his in Life and Death; and likewise our Time and Talents (as far as we shall think it our Duty) to the Glory of his Name, and support of his Interest. Again,

3. We give ourselves to one another according to the Will of God to be a Part or Branch of the vissible Church of Christ here upon Earth: accounting it our Privilege and greatest Honour to establish a Church to God in a Place where it never was before.

4. AND as such in the Name, Fear & Strength of JEHOVAH, we desire and it is our unfeigned Intention, To strive together for the faith of the Gospel: That is to say, The Doctrines of Grace in their several Branches; as far as we can see them in the Word of God and other useful Books: particularly, The Confession of Faith, as it was published by our baptized Brethren, in the Year 1689.

5. Moreover, in the same Strength, we will endeavour to support and practice the Ordinances of the Gospel in their Apostolick purity, taking the Word of God our chief Rule in this & all other Things.

6. [?] we earnestly desire, pray and firmly resolve, to walk in love with one another, and as far as possible, without offence toward those without: and in the practice of Every other Duty to God and Man tho' it has not been mentioned here; desire we do & endeavour we will to spread and adorn the Interest and ways of the Lord and Saviour Jesus Christ. With fervent and constant Prayers for the Influences of his Spirit, and rich Communications of his Grace to assist us here in: We do in the presence of the ever Blessed Trinity; The Angels of Heaven & this Congregation sincerely, uprightly and religiously give the right Hand of felowship to one another, and set our Names to the above Articles; Saying

So help me God! Amen

Source: National Library of Wales Ms. 1102B.

* * * * *

WREXHAM (CLWYD), 1773

ISAIAH Chap. 44th v. 5th.

One shall say, I am the Lord's; and another shall call himself by the name of Jacob; and another shall subscribe with his hand unto the Lord, and surname himself by the name of Israel.

JEREMIAH 50th v. 4, 5.

In those days and in that time saith the Lord, the children of Israel shall come, they and the children of Judah together, going and weeping; they shall go, and seek the Lord their God. They shall ask the way to Zion with their faces thitherward saying, come: and let us join ourselves to the Lord in a perpetual covenant that shall not be forgotten.

REVELATION 3d. v. 2d, 3d.

Be watchful and strengthen the things which remain that are ready to die – Remember therefore how thou hast received and heard, and hold fast and repent.

We, the underwritten, members of the Baptist Independent Church in Wrexham professing the belief of the doctrines of free, sovereign, and efficacious grace, do acknowledge the riches of that grace of God in providing a Saviour for us wretched sinners, even the Lord Jesus Christ: his goodness in sending the Gospel to us, at the ends of the earth; giving us some experience of the power of that Gospel in our souls (through the sacred operations of His Holy Spirit), humbling, comforting, charging, renewing us, calling us to be a part of His church in this world; and fixing a pastor over us.

And we do now in the name and in the fear of God, give up ourselves to the Lord and to one another by the will of God; desiring to walk together in church fellowship according to the rules of the Gospel, that is to say – conscientiously to sanctify the Lord's Day; to attend on the public preaching of the Word and the administration of the ordinances of Christ, church-meetings and meetings of prayer, unless some unavoidable hindrance prevent, to walk with and watch over one another in love; endeavouring in the strength of divine grace to maintain the unity of the Spirit in the bond of peace, to keep up the life of religion in our own souls, the exercise of daily prayer in private and in our families (not forgetting, at such seasons, the peace and prosperity of Zion, and of our own church and pastor in particular); and to walk uprightly and circumspectly in our own families and before the world, that others may see our good works, and may glorify our Father who is in heaven. Amen!

Following the covenant is the further declaration signed by members subsequently admitted to the church:

We, the underwritten, having been (at our request with a view to the glory of God and the comfort and edification of our own souls) proposed and admitted members of this Christian church, and having had recited to us the covenant within agreed to; do hereby testify our hearty and unfeigned assent to the solemn profession of faith and experience therein made; earnestly desiring in the strength of divine grace, to give ourselves up to this church in the Lord, to conform ourselves to the several regulations therein laid down from the Word of God and to walk with the other members in Christian fellowship and love according to the rules of the Gospel. Amen.

In 1776 the following additional covenant for Paedobaptist members of the church was agreed upon at a church meeting:

We the underwritten being Independents believing the baptism of infants, yet entertaining a Christian affection for our Brethren who believe adult baptism only, and being desirous of communicating with them at the table of the Lord, do hereby declare (at our entrance into this Church) that it shall, thro' grace, be our prayer, and our endeavour to walk with them in Brotherly-love and Christian fellowship; maintaining the Unity of the Spirit in the Bond of peace; and in case of the removal of the present or any future Pastor, this Church should become vacant, that then, we will consent to the settlement of a minister of the Baptist persuasion over it, and by no means seek to prevent or disturb such settlement; and this we think reasonable, considering that there is a Paedobaptist congregation in this Town; the Minister of which may admit the infants of such as desire it, to what we think their privilege; and that it would not be equitable to deprive our Baptist Brethren of a minister who may administer the ordinance of Baptism to them, in the way that they think most agreeable to the Word of God.

Source: G. V. Price, *The 'Old Meeting': The History of the Chester Street Baptist Church, Wrexham* (Wrexham, n.d.), 200, 209-11.

* * * * *

CAPEL Y FFIN (POWYS), 1784

At our Church Meeting June 2d 1784. We agree to make our Covenant as a Church with each other; in the name, & in the fear of the Lord; in His strength, as followeth. that is to say First if a Brother or Sister shall be found guilty of giveing a private offence to a fellow member, that such offended member, is to behave to the offender according to the Rule given in St. Matt. Chap 18. 15. 16. 17 verses. Secondly not to Neglect or forsake the Assembling of our Selves together on our Publick and more private prayer Meetings, but in love to convince, chasten, instruct, Sympathize, Comfort, bear each other's burden, And pray with and for one another, Heb 10.25. Thirdly that we or any of us are not to disclose the weakness and imperfection of the Church or any [of] our fellow Members, as we are instructed in 2 Sam Chap 1.20 verse. Fourthly to strive to observe & keep discipline in every part thereof in the Church of the living God according to His own directions. Fifthly that each of us shall according to our power strive to support the Ministry of the Gospel among us in our day & generation.

Source: National Library of Wales Ms. 182A.

LLANBRYN-MAIR (POWYS), 1798

A Church Covenant agreed upon by the Congregational Society of non-conformist protestants in Llanbrynmair.

As a Church of the living God, and members of the Lord Jesus Christ, whom alone we acknowledge Head of the Church, and by the help of the Holy Spirit, we bind ourselves and make a covenant with the Lord, and with one another in the following matters:

1. Regarding the points of our faith we assert the doctrines contained in the Catechism of the Assembly in accordance with the word of God.

2. We promise to strive against every sin and all occasions that appear likely to lead us into sin.

3. We promise to practice with constant diligence all the means, public and private, that God has commanded, namely, to pray, to meditate, to read, to listen to the word and to partake of communion, so as to build up ourselves and one another in grace and holiness.

4. We promise to strive conscientiously to uphold and to exercise such discipline in the House of God as is in accordance with His holy word.

5. We promise that if we do anything deserving of rebuke in the opinion of the Church, to submit to such rebuke as appears meet to the Church.

6. We promise to consult the Church when contemplating taking any important step, especially marriage; and we agree that it is the bounden duty of every church member not to carry on a friendship with any person with a view to marriage, without first of all consulting the Church, and that neglect of this duty in itself deserves rebuke.

7. We promise that we shall not harbour evil thoughts concerning one another without conscientiously ascertaining if we have just cause, and that we shall not believe every tale we hear about one another without sufficient testimony, and especially that we shall not slander one another, but rather that we shall conceal one another's faults in so far as we are able to do so with a good conscience.

8. We promise according to our gifts and opportunities, to do our utmost to build up one another in the Lord, that is, to pray and keep watch over one another, to be ready to give the best advice and guidance that we can to one another, and to behave kindly and forgivingly to one another according to the law of Christ.

9. Whatsoever be our family circumstances or at anytime may be, we promise to strive to fulfil every duty appertaining to our family life in a conscientious manner according to the word of God.

10. We promise carefully to refrain from repeating before unbelievers what is done or spoken in the Church lest we should be guilty of giving that which is holy to dogs and casting pearls before swine.

11. We promise that we shall contribute conscientiously and faithfully, according to our circumstances, towards the sustenance of the cause of the Lord in our midst.

12. We promise to do as much good as we can to every man in every station, and, through sober, honest, just, helpful and meek conversation, do our utmost to win others to the faith.

Source: National Library of Wales Ms. 1465C. The English translation is to be found in *Montgomeryshire Collections*, lii (1951-2), 68-9. The covenant was published in Welsh in *Y Cylchgrawn Efengylaidd* (Medi-Rhagfyr, 1972).

Since we devoutly hope, that God has called us by his grace, we feel an obligation to devote ourselves, in a public manner, to God, and his service; and as we prefer to be embodied into a Church, rather than to unite with any other Church, we hope that ministers and Churches will recognize us as such.

We now, in the most deliberate, and public manner, dedicate ourselves to God in church fellowship and communion, according to the rule of his revealed word. We are also determined, and we vow, that by divine aid, we will be stedfast in the faith, 'walk in all the commandments and ordinances of the Lord,' hear his word, trust in his promises, and serve him and each other according to the laws and institutions of his house.

Our purpose and aim in all this are, the glory of God, and our own edification, the increase of the kingdom of Christ, and the good of all mankind; and we earnestly pray that our dependence may be placed on the direction and aid of the Spirit of God.

Source: W. H. Lewis, *David Peter, Memoir of the Life and Labours of the Rev. David Peter* (London: Longman, Brown, Green and Longmans, 1846), 142-3.

THE TABERNACLE, PORTH.

THE CHURCH COVENANT

— OR —

The Conditions of Church Membership.

1.--Faithful attendance at the meetings of the Church. (Heb. x. 25; Acts ii. 41, 42).

2.--Faithful financial support of the work of the Church, both at home and abroad. (1 Cor. xvi. 2; 2 Cor. viii. 1-4).

3.--Faithful interest in the spiritual welfare of the Church as a whole and of its individual Members. (Eph. iv. 32; Heb. x. 24; Gal. vi. 1; Rom. xiv. 7; 1 Cor. viii. 13).

4.--Faithful regard to the sacred character of the affairs of the Church. (John xvii. 14; James iv. 4; 1 John ii. 15).

5.--Faithful submission to, and co-operation with the decisions of the Church. (John xvii. 22; Eph. iv. 3; Phil. ii. 3).

Appreciating the great privilege of fellowship in the Church of the Lord Jesus Christ.

Clearly realising that membership in the above Church is granted me on the above express conditions which I have carefully read and thoroughly understand, and

Relying on the Holy Spirit's ministry to me of the grace of the Lord Jesus Christ.

I, ..., HERETO DELIBERATELY SET MY HAND in token of my firm purpose and sincere promise to faithfully observe them all, and,

I further agree that if, for some reason, judged by the Church to be insufficient, I fail to observe them, the Church will be justified in regarding my right to continue membership therein to be forfeited.

Signed as in the Lord's Presence..

Witnessed by..

Date..192

Photographic reproduction of the printed Church Covenant of Tabernacle Baptist Church at Porth in the Rhondda Valley (see page 46)

NOTES

1. *Confession of Faith, of the Calvinistic Methodists . . . of Wales* (1823; English translation, Caernarfon: D. O'Brien Owen for the General Assembly, 1900), 56.
2. Among the best expositions of the subject are John Murray, *The Covenant of Grace: A Biblico-Theological Study* (London: Tyndale Press, 1954) and A. W. Pink, *The Divine Covenants* (Grand Rapids: Baker, 1973). More recent volumes include O. Palmer Robertson, *The Christ of the Covenants* (Phillipsburg, New Jersey: Presbyterian and Reformed, 1980), William J. Dumbrell, *Covenant and Creation: An Old Testament Covenantal Theology* (Exeter: Paternoster, 1984) and T. E. McComiskey, *The Covenants of Promise* (Grand Rapids: Baker, 1985). A useful discussion in Welsh is R. Tudur Jones, 'Athrawiaeth y Cyfamodau', *Y Traethodydd*, CV, 456 (Gorffennaf 1950), 118-26.
3. John Murray, *Collected Writings* (Edinburgh: Banner of Truth Trust, 1977), II, 49.
4. This, of course, is the significance of the preamble to the Ten Commandments in Exodus 20:2.
5. 'Covenant', in J. D. Douglas (ed.), *The New Bible Dictionary* (London: Inter-Varsity Fellowship, 1962), 267.
6. Geoffrey Thomas, 'Becoming a Christian – Covenant Theology: A Historical Survey', in *Becoming a Christian*, papers read at the 1972 Westminster Conference, 5-21; Jens G. Moller, 'The Beginnings of Puritan Covenant Theology', *Journal of Ecclesiastical History*, XIV, 1 (April 1963), 46-67.
7. Champlin Burrage, *The Early English Dissenters* (Cambridge: Cambridge University Press, 1912), II, 81-2; R. Tudur Jones, *Vavasor Powell* (Abertawe: Gwasg John Penry, 1971), 92-5; Griffith Jones, *The Christian Covenant, or the Baptismal Vow, as Stated in Our Church Catechism* (2nd edition; London, 1762).
8. R. Tudur Jones, *John Elias: Prince amongst Preachers* (Bridgend: Evangelical Library of Wales, 1975), 20-2. Perhaps the best-known hymns are 'Cyfamod hedd' by Edward Jones, Maes-y-plwm (1761-1836), and 'Y Cyfamod Di-sigl' (reaching its climax in the verse 'Y Gŵr a fu gynt o dan hoelion') by Hugh Derfel Hughes (1816-90). A covenant by Edward Jones's son, Daniel, made in 1829 when he was fifteen years old, is to be found in J. E. Caerwyn Williams, *Edward Jones, Maes-y-plwm* (Dinbych: Gwasg Gee, 1962), 20.
9. Moller, *Journal of Ecclesiastical History* (1963), 65-7.
10. C. H. Spurgeon, *The Early Years* (1897; republished, London: Banner of Truth Trust, 1962), 125.
11. J. B. Williams, *The Lives of Philip and Matthew Henry* (1698 and 1828; republished in one volume, Edinburgh: Banner of Truth Trust, 1974), 'Matthew Henry', 5.
12. Cf. Eifion Evans, *Two Welsh Revivalists: Humphrey Jones, Dafydd Mor-*

gan and the 1859 Revival in Wales (Bridgend: Evangelical Library of Wales, 1985), 31; Edward Morgan (ed.), *Letters of Rev. Griffith Jones, Llanddowror* (London, 1832), 15. Spurgeon was of the opinion that unrepentant sinners were in fact in implicit covenant with hell and challenged them to set out their covenants in black and white in order that they should realize the enormity of their rejection of God's mercy: *Metropolitan Tabernacle Pulpit*, 26 (1880; republished, London: Banner of Truth Trust, 1971), 441-2.

13. H. J. Hughes, *Life of Howell Harris* (Newport and London: Jones and Nisbet, 1892), 10.
14. *Ibid.*, 12-13.
15. *Works* (1834; republished, Edinburgh: Banner of Truth Trust, 1974), I, xiv, xxi, xxv.
16. Edward Morgan, *A Brief History of the Life and Labours of the Rev. T. Charles A.B.* (London, 1828), 117-18 .
17. Edward Matthews, *Bywgraffiad y Parch. Thos. Richard, Abergwaen* (Abertawe, 1863), 179-88; W. H. Peter, *Memoir of the Life and Labours of the Rev. David Peter* (London: Longman, Brown, Green and Longmans, 1846), 144-9. One of Richard's covenants is reproduced in Appendix A.
18. Williams, *Philip and Matthew Henry*, 'Matthew Henry', 76. Further examples are to be found in Appendix A.
19. E. Morgan, *T. Charles*, 52; Trebor Lloyd Evans, *Lewis Edwards: Ei Fywyd a'i Waith* (Abertawe: Gwasg John Penry, 1967), 29-30. David Brainerd was also among those who made a covenant on such an occasion (Jonathan Edwards, *Works*, II, 347).
20. Thomas Charles, *Hyfforddwr yn Egwyddorion y Grefydd Gristionogol ['The Christian Instructor']* (1807; English translation, Caernarfon: D. O'Brien Owen, n.d.), Q.229; George Lewis, *Drych Ysgrythyrol, neu Gorph o Dduwinyddiaeth* (Wrexham: Hughes & Son, n.d.), 473; Jonathan Edwards, *Works*, II, 411.
21. Williams, *Philip and Matthew Henry*, 'Philip Henry', 83-4.
22. S. Pearce Carey, *William Carey* (London: Carey Press, 1934), 117-18, 262; John Telford, *The Methodist Hymn-Book Illustrated in History and Experience* (seventh edition, London: Epworth Press, 1959), 355. See also Leslie F. Church, *More About the Early Methodist People* (London: Epworth Press, 1949), 276. From one aspect, of course, marriage is itself a covenant relationship – see Horton Davies, *Worship and Theology in England: From Andrewes to Baxter and Fox, 1603-1690* (Princeton: Princeton University Press, 1975), 419.
23. Richard Bennett, 'Howell Davies', *Journal of the Calvinistic Methodist Historical Society*, III, 4 (June 1918), 96-7; John Bunyan, *Pilgrim's Progress* (1676; republished, Edinburgh: Banner of Truth Trust, 1977), 110. For other examples, see Jonathan Edwards, *Works*, I, lxii; Richard Baxter, *Autobiography* (London: Dent, 1931), 269. A more recent example is to be found in Iain H. Murray, *David Martyn Lloyd-Jones: The*

First Forty Years 1899-1939 (Edinburgh: Banner of Truth Trust, 1982), 241-2.

24. W. Morgan, *Cofiant . . . Christmas Evans* (Caerdydd: Ll. Jenkins, 1839), 35-7, 50, 53-5; Paxton Hood, *Christmas Evans: The Preacher of Wild Wales* (London: Hodder and Stoughton, 1883), 78-80, 277-80. Two of these covenants are reproduced in Appendix A.
25. David Jones, *Hanes y Bedyddwyr yn Neheubarth Cymru* (Caerfyrddin, 1839), 80-1.
26. Philip Doddridge, *Works* (London, 1803), II, 146-7. This work was published in Welsh for the first time in 1788 and had no little influence in Wales – see, for example, D. Jones, *Hanes y Bedyddwyr*, 80.
27. Joseph Alleine, *An Alarm to the Unconverted* (1671; republished, London: Banner of Truth Trust, 1964), 117-20. Alleine also published a separate *Directions for Covenanting with God* – see Charles Stanford, *Joseph Alleine: His Companions & Times* (London: Jackson, Walford and Hodder, 1864), 393.
28. William Guthrie, *The Christian's Great Interest* (1658; republished, London: Banner of Truth Trust, 1969), 169.
29. John Jones, *Cofiant . . . y Parch Michael Roberts, Pwllheli* (Pwllheli: R. Owen, 1883), 83-4 – the covenant is included in Appendix A; S. Pearce Carey, *Samuel Pearce: The Baptist Brainerd* (London: Carey Press, n.d.), 66. Cf. D. Jones, *Hanes y Bedyddwyr*, 82, and L.F. Church, *More Early Methodists*, 276.
30. M. H. Lee (ed.), *Diaries and Letters of Philip Henry MA* (London: Kegan Paul, Trench, 1882), 160-1.
31. *Christian's Great Interest*, 174-6.
32. Geoffrey F. Nuttall, *Richard Baxter* (London: Nelson, 1965), 53; John Jones, *Cofiant . . . Michael Roberts*, 13.
33. C. H. Spurgeon, *Morning by Morning* (London: Passmore and Alabaster, 1865), 115. For examples in practice, see J. Horsfall Turner (ed.), *Oliver Heywood: His Autobiography, Diaries, Anecdote, and Event-Books* (Brighouse and Bingley: J. H. Turner, 1882-85), I, 300-2, 307-32; III, 123-4, 221f. Compare also E. G. Millward, *Detholion o Ddyddiadur Eben Fardd* (Caerdydd: Gwasg Prifysgol Cymru, 1968), 109-11, 137-8. There is a particularly moving covenant written by a minister who had fallen into sin and who desired to return to his Lord in *Y Dysgedydd*, V (1826), 289-91.
34. Thomas Boston, *Human Nature in its Fourfold State* (1720; republished, London: Banner of Truth Trust, 1964), 273-5. This work was published in Welsh in 1821.
35. Robert Mackenzie, *John Brown of Haddington* (1918; republished, London: Banner of Truth Trust, 1964), 21, 25-6, 224.
36. J. C. Ryle, *Christian Leaders of the Eighteenth Century* (1885: republished, Edinburgh: Banner of Truth Trust, 1978), 134.
37. Edward Matthews, *Bywgraffiad . . . Thos Richard*, 185; cf. his covenant included in Appendix A. See L. F. Church, *More Early Methodists*, 275,

for an example of boldness in covenanting.

38. *Memoirs of Rev. Charles G. Finney, Written by Himself* (New York: A. S. Barnes, 1876), 63; William G. McLoughlin, Jr., *Modern Revivalism: Charles Grandison Finney to Billy Graham* (New York: Ronald, 1959), 156-7.
39. Eifion Evans, *When He is Come: An Account of the 1858-60 Revival in Wales* (Bala: Evangelical Movement of Wales, 1959), 104 – a revised edition of this book, with an index (but without the notes which contain the decision card), is published by the Evangelical Press of Wales under the title *Revival Comes to Wales.*
40. [Edward Bagshaw?], *The Life and Death of Mr. Vavasor Powell* ([London]: 1671), 113-14.
41. E. Morgan, *T. Charles*, 29.
42. Henry Bettenson (ed.), *Documents of the Christian Church* (Oxford: Oxford University Press, 1943), 5.
43. E. Morgan (ed.), *Letters of . . . Griffith Jones*, 87; cf. 282; Henry Hughes, *Hanes Diwygiadau Crefyddol Cymru* (Caernarfon: Cwmni'r Wasg Genedlaethol Gymreig, [1906]), 254.
44. Michael R. Watts, *The Dissenters: From the Reformation to the French Revolution* (Oxford: Clarendon Press, 1978), 460-1. Jonathan Edwards's *Humble Attempt* is included in *Works*, II, 278-312.
45. Hughes, *Hanes Diwygiadau*, 354; E. Evans, *When He is Come*, 32-3, 72.
46. Eifion Evans, *The Welsh Revival of 1904* (third edition, Bridgend: Evangelical Press of Wales, 1987), 169 – F. B. Meyer claimed that these meetings, held at his instigation, were ultimately responsible for the events of 1904-5, but his claims were strongly opposed by Cynddylan Jones (*ibid.*, 169-70); Iain Murray, *D. M. Lloyd-Jones*, I, 199. A still more recent example is the covenant to pray for revival for one hour every Saturday evening, entered into by those attending the Ministers' Conference organized by the Evangelical Movement of Wales in 1983, and inspired by Jonathan Edwards's *Humble Attempt;* see *Evangelical Magazine of Wales*, XX, 4 (August-September 1983), 4.
47. Burrage, *Dissenters*, I, 288-90, 304. The first known example is that at Stoke (Suffolk) around 1558 (*ibid.*, 73). Among well-known figures who engaged in this practice were John Robinson (leader of the Pilgrim Fathers), Richard Rogers, John Eliot (the 'Apostle to the Indians'), John Cotton, John Rogers of Dedham and, possibly, Thomas Hooker – see *ibid.*, 289; Patrick Collinson, *The Elizabethan Puritan Movement* (London: Jonathan Cape, 1967), 381-2; Edmund S. Morgan, *Visible Saints: The History of a Puritan Idea* (New York: New York University Press, 1963), 77-8; Frank Shuffelton, *Thomas Hooker* (Princeton: Princeton University Press, 1977), 170-1.
48. Champlin Burrage, *The Church Covenant Idea: Its Origin and Its Development* (Philadelphia: American Baptist Publication Society, 1904), 13-25.
49. T. H. L. Parker, *John Calvin: A Biography* (London: J. M. Dent, 1975),

63, 65.
50. Burrage, *Covenant*, 26-33; *idem*, *Dissenters*, I, 74, 76-8.
51. Michael R. Watts, *Dissenters*, 25-6; Burrage, *Dissenters*, I, 80, 89-93.
52. Burrage, *Dissenters*, I, 97-9, 123-8, 230, 300, 310.
53. *Ibid.*, 314.
54. Examples of these covenants may be found in Burrage, *Covenant*, and Geoffrey F. Nuttall, *Visible Saints: The Congregational Way, 1640-1660* (Oxford: Blackwell, 1957). *The Axminster Ecclesiastica, 1660-1698*, ed. K. W. H. Howard (Sheffield: Gospel Tidings Publications, 1976) is a thoroughly interesting account of a church which not only had a covenant but frequently renewed it during a period of spiritual leanness and persecution. See also R. Tudur Jones, 'The Church Covenant in Classical Congregationalism', *The Presbyter*, Vll, 4 (1949), 9-20. Among the more accessible doctrinal discussions of the role of the covenant in the church by the Puritan authors is John Owen, 'The True Nature of a Gospel Church', in *Works* (1850-53 edition; republished, London: Banner of Truth Trust, 1968), XVI, 25-30.
55. Burrage, *Covenant*, 54, 86, 93-4. One of the most significant events in early Baptist history in New England was the formation in 1663 of a church at Swansey, Massachusetts, on the basis of a covenant. This church had its origins in the Baptist cause founded by John Miles at Ilston, Gower, in 1649. A facsimile copy of the covenant is to be found in the National Library of Wales at Aberystwyth – NLW Ms. 9108D: Ilston Register – and is being prepared for publication by the Library. See also Burrage, *Covenant*, 173-6.
56. Perry Miller, *The New England Mind: The Seventeenth Century* (New York: Macmillan, 1939), 439-40. Miller, while displaying vast erudition on the subject of early Christianity in New England, is hardly sympathetic towards his subject. Some of the early covenants are to be found in Williston Walker, *The Creeds and Platforms of Congregationalism* (New York: Scribner's, 1893), and the practice is explained and defended by such prominent leaders as John Cotton, in *The Way of the Churches of Christ in New-England* (London, 1645), 2-4, and Thomas Hooker, in *Survey of the Summe of Church Discipline* (London, 1648), part 1, 45-55. See also Stephen Brachlow, 'John Robinson and the Separatist Ideal', in *The Puritan Experiment in the New World*, papers read at the 1976 Westminster Conference, 5-18.
57. Burrage, *Dissenters*, II, 81-2; David Williams (ed.), *John Penry: Three Treatises Concerning Wales* (Cardiff: University of Wales Press, 1960), xxiv-xxv. Examples of covenant undertakings at this church are given in L. H. Carlson (ed.), *The Writings of John Greenwood and Henry Barrow, 1591-1593* (London: George Allen and Unwin for the Sir Halley Stewart Trust, 1970), 368-70, 380-1.
58. Nuttall, *Visible Saints*, 34-6, 47, 41; cf. R. Geraint Gruffydd *'In That Gentile Country . . . ': The Beginnings of Puritan Nonconformity in Wales* (Bridgend: Evangelical Library of Wales, 1976), 15, and 'William

Wroth a Chychwyniadau Anghydffurfiaeth yng Nghymru', in *Ysgrif-au Diwinyddol II,* ed. Noel A. Gibbard (Pen-y-bont ar Ogwr: Gwasg Efengylaidd Cymru, 1988), 132. The Broadmead covenants of 1640 and 1645 are recorded in Burrage, *Covenant*, 151-3.

59. *Spirituall Experiences, of Sundry Beleevers . . . with the recommendation by Vavasor Powell* (London, 1653), cited in R. T. Jones, *Presbyter*, VII (1949), 16-17; cf. Matthias Maurice, *Social Religion Exemplify'd, in an Account of the First Settlement of Christianity in the City of Caerludd* [=London] (London, 1737), 94-9. It is worth comparing these accounts with that of the formation of an actual church, such as Caerleon in 1771 (National Library of Wales Deposit Ms. 1102B), included in Appendix B.
60. Nuttall, *Visible Saints*, 78; Horton Davies, *The Worship of the English Puritans* (London: Dacre Press, 1948), 86, 94, 274; J. Morgan Jones, 'Cyfamodau Eglwys Llanbrynmair', *Y Cofiadur*, 2 (Mawrth 1924), 27, 39.
61. In England the Baptists seem to have been somewhat slower to adopt the church covenant (Burrage, *Covenant*, 62-78, 113-21). Examples of Baptist covenants in England may be found in W. T. Whitley, 'Church Covenants', *Baptist Quarterly*, VII, 1 (January 1935), 227-34.
62. National Library of Wales Deposit Ms. 409B: Llanwenarth Register.
63. National Library of Wales Deposit Ms. 127A: Rhydwilym Register; Ms. 369A: Mynydd-bach Register. The latter is reproduced in Appendix B. Members at Mynydd-bach undertook some form of covenant engagement in 1666, but the earliest extant document is the 1759 renewal of the 1700 covenant (National Library of Wales Ms. 369A).
64. For these and other examples, see D. Jones, *Hanes y Bedyddwyr*, 475 , 665, 144, 148, 244, 229-30.
65. J. M. Jones, *Cofiadur*, 2 (1924), 25-37. These covenants are reproduced in Appendix B.
66. G. V. Price, *The 'Old Meeting': The History of the Chester Street Baptist Church, Wrexham* (Wrexham, n.d.), 209-11.
67. D. Jones, *Hanes y Bedyddwyr*, 762; John Davies, *Arch y Cyfammod* (Llanelli, 1840), 450-61; *idem, Clorian y Cyssegr, neu y Cristion Biblaidd* (Caerfyrddin, 1845), 95-114. The latest covenants among denominational churches in Wales known to the present writer are those of the Baptist churches at Hanbury Road, Bargoed (1896 and *circa* 1901) and Bethel, Bedwas (1901) – see Brynmor P. Jones, *Sowing Beside All Waters: The Baptist Heritage of Gwent* (Gwent Baptist Association, 1985), 138-9, 146, 134.
68. A few examples may be found in D. Jones, *Hanes y Bedyddwyr*, 677, and in B. P. Jones, *Sowing Beside All Waters*, 143-7.
69. Azariah Shadrach, *Cerbyd o Goed Libanus, at yr Hyn y Chwanegwyd Hanes Byr o Fywyd yr Awdwr* (Aberystwyth, 1840), 199, 190.
70. J. Morgan Jones, 'Hen Gyfamodau Eglwysi'r Annibynwyr', *Undeb yr*

Annibynwyr Cymreig: Adroddiad Cyfarfodydd yr Undeb ym Mrynaman 1916 (Abertawe: Y Llyfrfa, 1916). R. Tudur Jones has shown that the speaker also misunderstood or misrepresented the essential doctrinal basis of the covenant – *Presbyter*, VII (1949), 20. For the decline in England, see Burrage, *Covenant*, 148, 166.

71. Brynmor P. Jones, *The King's Champions* (The author, 1968), 184-7; second, enlarged edition, with index (The author, 1986), 192-5. (Despite its independent stance and much tension in its relationship with the denomination in that period, Tabernacle did not formally leave the Baptist Union.) Some of the recently-formed independent evangelical churches in Wales, such as the Welsh-language evangelical church in Cardiff (established 1979), have church covenants.
72. The two books bearing this same title, one by Nuttall and the other by Morgan, are most helpful on this whole subject.
73. The story of the Covenanters has been told many times, but S. M. Houghton has contributed a particularly useful short summary of the historical background in Jock Purves, *Fair Sunshine* (London: Banner of Truth Trust, 1968), 195-203.
74. National Library of Wales Ms. 369A; Price, *The 'Old Meeting'*, 199.
75. Cited in Morgan, *Visible Saints*, 29, 41; E. Brooks Holifield, *The Covenant Sealed: The Development of Puritan Sacramental Theology in Old and New England, 1570-1720* (New Haven: Yale University Press, 1974), 64. See also T. Hooker, *Survey of the Summe of Church-Discipline*, part 1, 46.
76. Perry Miller, *The New England Mind: From Colony to Province* (Cambridge, Mass.: Harvard University Press, 1953), 73; S. P. Carey, *William Carey*, 61-2.
77. Burrage, *Dissenters*, I, 90-1.
78. National Library of Wales Ms. 371B: Mynydd-bach/Capel Isaac Church Book, published in *Y Cofiadur*, 17 (March 1947), 7-50; E. Lewis Evans, *Capel Isaac* (Llandysul, 1950), 69. See Morgan, *Visible Saints*, 88-93, for the normal method of admitting members in New England, and cf. Burrage, *Covenant*, 213-16.
79. Robert G. Pope, *The Half-Way Covenant: Church Membership in Puritan New England* (Princeton: Princeton University Press, 1969); David Boorman, 'The Halfway Covenant', in *The Puritan Experiment in the New World*, papers read at the 1976 Westminster Conference, 73-102. One of the most prominent opponents of the 'Half-way Covenant' was Richard Blinman, a native of Chepstow who was an active member of the Puritan community in New England between 1640 and 1659 – see E. Stanley John, 'Richard Blinman (1608-1681), Piwritan Cymreig: Bedydd Babanod', in E. Stanley John (ed.), *Y Gair a'r Genedl: Cyfrol Deyrnged i R. Tudur Jones* (Abertawe: Gwasg John Penry, 1986), 112-26.
80. Burrage, *Covenant*, 64-78, 84-5. Particular Baptists in England seem to have adopted covenants more extensively than General Baptists

(*ibid.*, 156).

81. *Ibid.*, 113-21, 124-5; *idem*, *Dissenters*, I, 261-2; A. S. P. Woodhouse, *Puritanism and Liberty* (London: Dent, 1938; reprinted, 1965), [74].
82. The church covenant is not mentioned at all in the standard work by T. M. Bassett, *The Welsh Baptists* (Swansea: Ilston House, 1977).
83. *Cerbyd o Goed Libanus*, 199. A member of the Baptist church at Capel-y-ffin, Breconshire, was excluded from the fellowship in 1793 for breaking his covenant through his non-attendance at the meetings of the church (National Library of Wales Deposit Ms. 182A: Capel-y-ffin Register).
84. B. P. Jones, *King's Champions*, 186-7; second ed., 194-5.
85. Joshua Thomas, *Hanes y Bedyddwyr yn mhlith y Cymry*, ed. B. Davies (Pontypridd: B. Davies, 1865), 547-8. The relationship between the church covenant and the doctrinal stance of Welsh Independents is discussed in Noel Gibbard, 'Yr Annibynwyr a Chredo', *Ysgrifau Diwinyddol I*, ed. Noel A. Gibbard (Pen-y-bont ar Ogwr: Gwasg Efengylaidd Cymru, 1979), 56-73.
86. NLW Ms. 409B; NLW Ms. 369A; J. M. Jones, *Cofiadur*, 2 (1924), 25, 28-30.
87. J. T. Jones, *Christmas Evans* (Llandysul: Gwasg Gomer, 1938), 24; B. P. Jones, *King's Champions*, 184; second ed., 192.
88. Pope, *Half-Way Covenant*, 120, 188-9, 240-5.
89. David D. Hall, *The Faithful Shepherd: A History of the New England Ministry in the Seventeenth Century* (Chapel Hill: University of North Carolina Press, 1972), 243-4; Jonathan Edwards, *Works*, I, lix-lx.
90. See Appendix B.
91. R. Tudur Jones, *Hanes Annibynwyr Cymru* (Abertawe: Undeb yr Annibynwyr Cymraeg, 1966), 271.
92. See Appendix B and further examples in other covenants reproduced there.
93. Joshua Thomas, *Hanes y Bedyddwyr*, 547-8. This subject is discussed in an American context in Larzer Ziff, 'The Social Bond of the Church Covenant', *American Quarterly*, X (1958), 454-62. Backslidden members who were subsequently restored were normally required to renew their original covenant undertakings – see, for example, National Library of Wales Ms. 371B: Mynydd-bach/Capel Isaac Church Book, p.23.
94. Holifield, *The Covenant Sealed*, 62-7, 76-7, 144-5, 181-2.
95. Price, *The 'Old Meeting'*, 199-200.
96. *Y Dysgedydd* (1824), 230.
97. Morgan, *Visible Saints*, 46, 146-150.
98. Iain H. Murray, *Jonathan Edwards: A New Biography* (Edinburgh: Banner of Truth Trust, 1987), 311-49.
99. *Corph o Dduwinyddiaeth*, 481. In some churches the covenant was read aloud before the partaking of the bread and wine – see Horton Davies, *Worship of the English Puritans*, 275.

100. *Clorian y Cyssegr*, 96-101; cf. Thomas Phillips, *Natur Cyfammod Eglwys* (Caerfyrddin, 1815), 8, 18-34.
101. Miller, *New England Mind: Seventeenth Century*, 450-2.
102. Cited in Woodhouse, *Puritanism and Liberty*, 300. There is no room here to discuss the significance of the covenant in political thought. For further information on the covenant and politics in the Puritan period, see *ibid.*, pp. [74] - [78].
103. National Library of Wales Ms. 409B.
104. Cf. Burrage, *Covenant*, 110, 212.
105. National Library of Wales Ms. 369A.
106. Cited in Miller, *New England Mind: Seventeenth Century*, 452.
107. It was far from uncommon for churches to engage (or re-engage) in covenant when choosing and ordaining their leaders – see, for example, National Library of Wales Ms. 371B, f.289; Matthias Maurice, *Social Religion*, 97.
108. *Y Dysgedydd* (1824), 230-1; cf. T. Phillips, *Natur Cyfammod Eglwys*, 16-17.
109. *Corph o Dduwinyddiaeth*, 445; cf. T. Phillips, *Natur Cyfammod Eglwys*, 17-18.
110. National Library of Wales Deposit Ms. 1102B: Caerleon Register.
111. Cited in Burrage, *Covenant*, 103-4. For the background to these objections, and the various replies to them, see R. P. Stearns, *The Strenuous Puritan: Hugh Peter, 1598-1660* (Urbana: University of Illinois Press, 1954), 211.
112. See, for example, *Y Dysgedydd* (1824), 140, 232; John Davies, *Arch y Cyfammod*, 453-4.
113. Woodhouse, *Puritanism and Liberty*, 299; Miller, *New England Mind: Seventeenth Century*, 438. For a modern attempt to find a scriptural basis for a church covenant, see Malcolm H. Watts, 'Why Have a Church Covenant?', *Reformation Today*, 88 (Nov.-Dec. 1985), 6-10.
114. *Traethodau Duwinyddol* (Wrecsam: Hughes a'i Fab, n.d.), 250.
115. *The Church of Christ* (1868; republished, Edinburgh: Banner of Truth Trust, 1974), I, 75-6; cf. 31-2. The relationship between the implicit and the explicit covenant is well discussed by Thomas Hooker in his *Survey of the Summe of Church-Discipline*, part 1, 47-9.
116. Miller, *New England Mind: Seventeenth Century*, 437; cf. Nuttall, *Visible Saints*, 78.
117. Cited in Williston Walker, *Creeds and Platforms*, 208.

INDEX

EVANGELICAL LIBRARY OF WALES SERIES

Series Editor: E. Wyn James

IN WELSH:

Nos. 1 & 2*	*John Elias – Pregethwr a Phendefig* (R. Tudur Jones)
No. 3	*Robert Roberts – Yr Angel o Glynnog* (Emyr Roberts & E. Wyn James)
No. 4*	*Ann Griffiths: Y Cyfrinydd Sylweddol* (Bobi Jones)
No. 5	*Elusen i'r Enaid: Arweiniad i Weithiau'r Piwritaniaid Cymreig, 1630-1689* (Noel Gibbard)
No. 6	*Islwyn: Y Dyn Bach Mawr* (Gwyn Davies)
No. 7	*Dadl Grefyddol Saunders Lewis ac W.J. Gruffydd* (John Emyr)
No. 8	*Yr Efengyl yn y Wladfa* (Robert Owen Jones)
No. 9	*Meddiannu Tir Immanuel: Cymru a Mudiad Cenhadol y Ddeunawfed Ganrif* (Dewi Arwel Hughes)

IN ENGLISH:

No. 1*	*Daniel Rowland – Man of Truth and Power* (Hywel R. Jones)
No. 2*	*John Elias – Prince Amongst Preachers* (R. Tudur Jones)
No. 3*	*'In that Gentile Country . . .': The Beginnings of Puritan Nonconformity in Wales* (R. Geraint Gruffydd)
No. 4*	*Walter Cradock: 'A New Testament Saint'* (Noel Gibbard)
No. 5*	*Christian Schools: Christianity and Education in Mid-Nineteenth-Century Wales and its Relevance for Today* (D. Eryl Davies)
No. 6*	*Revival and its Fruit* (Emyr Roberts & R. Geraint Gruffydd)
No. 7	*Martyn Lloyd-Jones: The Man and his Books* (Frederick & Elizabeth Catherwood)
No. 8*	*Two Welsh Revivalists: Humphrey Jones, Dafydd Morgan and the 1859 Revival in Wales* (Eifion Evans)
No. 9	*Covenanting with God* (Gwyn Davies)

**Out of print*